TypeScript Basics

Learn TypeScript from Scratch and Solidify Your Skills with Projects

Nabendu Biswas

Apress®

TypeScript Basics: Learn TypeScript from Scratch and Solidify Your Skills with Projects

Nabendu Biswas
Bhopal, India

ISBN-13 (pbk): 978-1-4842-9522-9   ISBN-13 (electronic): 978-1-4842-9523-6
https://doi.org/10.1007/978-1-4842-9523-6

Managing Director, Apress Media LLC: Welmoed Spahr
Acquisitions Editor: James Robinson-Prior
Development Editor: James Markham
Coordinating Editor: Gryffin Winkler
Copy Editor: Kezia Endsley

Cover image designed by eStudioCalamar

Distributed to the book trade worldwide by Apress Media, LLC, 1 New York Plaza, New York, NY 10004, U.S.A. Phone 1-800-SPRINGER, fax (201) 348-4505, e-mail orders-ny@springer-sbm.com, or visit www.springeronline.com. Apress Media, LLC is a California LLC and the sole member (owner) is Springer Science + Business Media Finance Inc (SSBM Finance Inc). SSBM Finance Inc is a **Delaware** corporation.

For information on translations, please e-mail booktranslations@springernature.com; for reprint, paperback, or audio rights, please e-mail bookpermissions@springernature.com.

Apress titles may be purchased in bulk for academic, corporate, or promotional use. eBook versions and licenses are also available for most titles. For more information, reference our Print and eBook Bulk Sales web page at http://www.apress.com/bulk-sales.

Any source code or other supplementary material referenced by the author in this book is available to readers on GitHub (https://github.com/Apress). For more detailed information, please visit https://www.apress.com/gp/services/source-code.

Paper in this product is recyclable

This book is affectionately dedicated to my wife and kid.

Table of Contents

About the Author ix

About the Technical Reviewer xi

Introduction xiii

Chapter 1: Getting Started 1

    Project Setup 1

    Summary...4

Chapter 2: TypeScript Basics 5

    The Number Type 5

    The String and Boolean Types..7

    Inference 7

    Objects 8

    Arrays..10

        Complex Arrays..11

    Functions 12

    Union Types 13

    Literal Types 14

    Enum Types 14

    Optionals Type...15

    Interfaces and Types 16

    Running the Code..18

    Summary...19

Chapter 3: The TypeScript Compiler 21

Watch Mode 21

Compiling an Entire Project..22

rootDir and outDir 26

Summary...27

Chapter 4: Classes and Interfaces..29

The Basics about Classes 29

Advanced Classes 34

Interface Basics 44

Summary...49

Chapter 5: Advanced Types 51

Initial Setup...51

Intersection Types 52

Type Guards and Discriminated Unions 53

Type Casting...56

Index Properties...58

Function Overloading 59

Nullish Coalescing..61

Summary...62

Chapter 6: Generics and Decorators...63

Initial Setup...63

Array and Promise Types..64

Generic Functions 65

Type Constraints..66

Generic Classes 68

Generic Utilities...69

Decorators Setup 69

Simple Decorators 71

Decorator Factories.. 73

Useful Decorators 74

Property Decorators 75

Summary.. 78

Chapter 7: Creating a To-do List Project with TypeScript 79

Initial Setup... 79

Creating the To-Do List.. 81

Summary.. 86

Chapter 8: Creating a Drag-and-Drop Project with TypeScript...........87

Initial Setup... 87

DOM Selection 89

Rendering a List.. 95

Filtering Logic 102

Abstract Class 107

Rendering Items.. 112

Draggable Items.. 115

Summary.. 122

Chapter 9: Improving the Drag-and-Drop Project...........................123

Changing to ES6 Modules 123

Using Webpack.. 134

Summary.. 140

Chapter 10: Creating a Party App in ReactJS with TypeScript 141

Party App...141

Listing People 142

Adding People 146

Summary...151

Chapter 11: Using React Redux with TypeScript 153

Setting Up the Project..153

Setting Up Redux 154

The Output 157

Summary...160

Index..161

About the Author

Nabendu Biswas is a full stack JavaScript developer. He has worked in the IT industry for the past 18 years for the world's top development firms and investment banks. He is a passionate tech blogger and YouTuber and he currently works as an Architect in an IT company at Bhopal. He is the author of five books, all published by Apress. His books cover Gatsby, MERN, and React Firebase.

About the Technical Reviewer

**Alexander Nnakwue** has a background in mechanical engineering. He is a senior software engineer with over seven years of experience in various industries, including payments, blockchain, and marketing technologies. He is a published author in professional JavaScript, as well as a technical writer and reviewer. Currently, he is working as a software engineer at Konecranes, helping the digital experience team with machine data and industrial cranes.

In his spare time, he loves to listen to music and enjoys the game of soccer. He currently lives in Helsinki, Finland with his lovely wife.

Introduction

TypeScript is revolutionizing how developers create JavaScript apps. It was built by Microsoft to fix the issues that came out of loose binding in JavaScript. Since JavaScript is a loosely typed language, a lot of issues ended up in the production apps. These issues were hard to track and took a lot of time to fix.

TypeScript is a superset of JavaScript, and it enables you to avoid type errors before they even occur. You can catch them in an IDE (Integrated Development Environment) like VS Code. The popular JavaScript frontend framework of Angular uses TypeScript by default. The most popular JavaScript frontend library called React also uses JavaScript by default.

This book first teaches you about TypeScript, and then you will use it in a ReactJS project. You will also use it with the JavaScript backend framework of NodeJS and learn how to create a React Redux project.

Introduction

CHAPTER 1

Getting Started

Welcome to *TypeScript Basics*, where you'll learn TypeScript from scratch and solidify your skills by creating some projects. TypeScript is a superset of JavaScript and was built by Microsoft to fix the issues of loose binding in JavaScript.

After learning the fundamentals of TypeScript in the first six chapters, you will use that information to create the following projects:

- A to-do list (Chapter 7)

- A drag-and-drop project (Chapters 8 and 9)

- A party app (Chapter 10)

- A React Redux TypeScript project (Chapter 11)

With TypeScript, you get all the new features of JavaScript, through which you can avoid type errors before they occur. The limitation of TypeScript is that browsers can't execute it.

Browsers only understand JavaScript, so TypeScript needs to be compiled to JavaScript. This chapter starts with the basic setup.

Project Setup

Open a new folder in VS Code and create a basic `index.html` file in it (see Listing 1-1). This example also refers to a JavaScript file called `main.js`.

© Nabendu Biswas 2023
N. Biswas, *TypeScript Basics*, https://doi.org/10.1007/978-1-4842-9523-6_1

Listing 1-1. Basic index.html File

```
<!DOCTYPE html>
<html lang="en">
<head>
    <meta charset="UTF-8">
    <meta name="viewport" content="width=device-width,
    initial-scale=1.0">
    <title>TypeScript Basics</title>
</head>
<body>
    <h1>TypeScript Basics</h1>
    <script src="main.js"></script>
</body>
</html>
```

Next, install TypeScript globally on your system with the following command. Add a sudo if you are using a Mac or Linux system.

```
1    npm i -g typescript
```

Now, create the main.ts file and add a simple console.log to it. The browser only understands JavaScript, so you have to change it to JavaScript using the tsc main.ts command. The tsc command runs the TypeScript compiler and converts the TypeScript file to JavaScript. This command will create a new main.js JavaScript file in the same directory. See Figure 1-1.

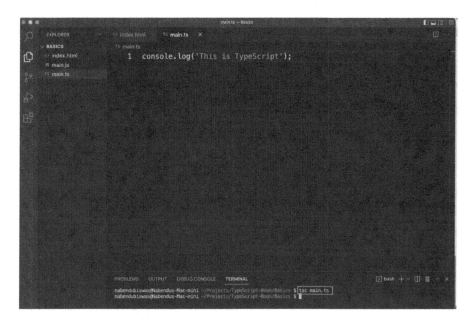

Figure 1-1. *Simple main.ts*

You will also be using the awesome extension of <u>Live Server</u> in this project (see Figure 1-2) so that you don't have to rerun the project after every change.

Figure 1-2. *Live Server*

3

Summary

In this introductory chapter, you completed the basic setup for TypeScript. You installed TypeScript globally and created basic HTML and TypeScript files and made them work together.

CHAPTER 2

TypeScript Basics

This chapter starts your TypeScript journey. Here, you will learn about different types and ways to use them in your projects. You will start with the number type, followed by the string and Boolean types. You will also learn about many more types and end by learning about interfaces.

The Number Type

Create an index.ts file in your earlier setup. Then add the code in Listing 2-1 to it. You have two variables—myNum and anotherNum. The code gives anotherNum the number type.

That means the myNum and anotherNum variables cannot take anything other than numbers.

Listing 2-1. Number Types

```
//Numbers
let myNum = 10;
let anotherNum: number = 20;

myNum = 12;
myNum = '12';

anotherNum = 30;
anotherNum = false;
```

© Nabendu Biswas 2023
N. Biswas, *TypeScript Basics*, https://doi.org/10.1007/978-1-4842-9523-6_2

If you hover your mouse over the error, you can see the real issues, as shown in Figures 2-1 and 2-2.

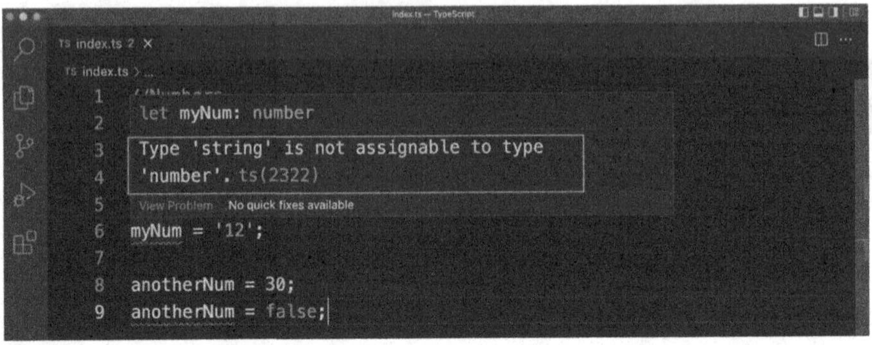

Figure 2-1. *Number issue*

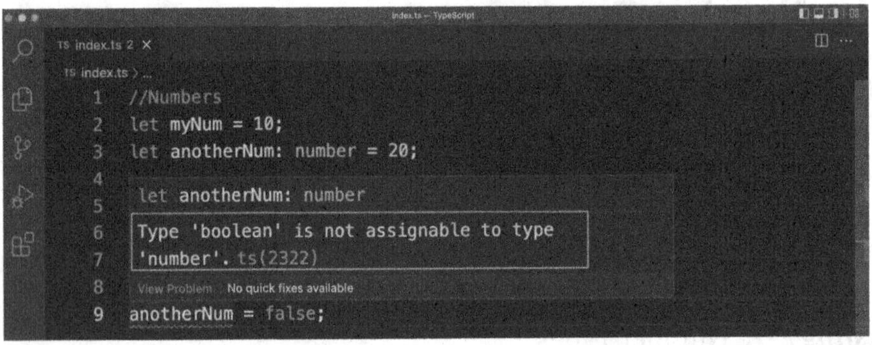

Figure 2-2. *Boolean issue*

As you can see in this example, even if you don't assign a type, TypeScript infers a type. Hover the mouse over myNum and it will show the number type. See Figure 2-3.

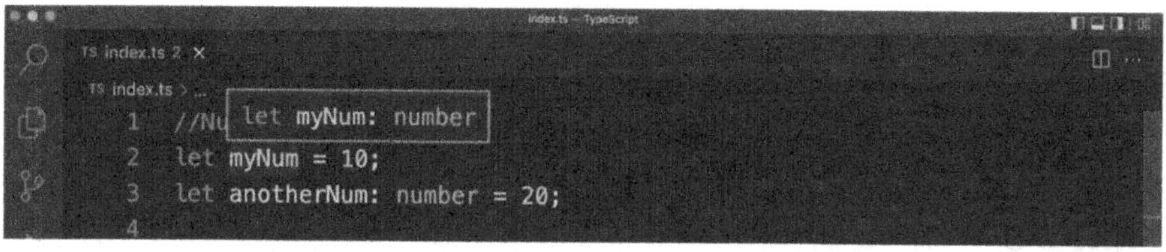

Figure 2-3. *TypeScript*

The String and Boolean Types

The same is true for the String and Boolean types. When you first assign a
type and then give the wrong type, you will get an error. Second, the types
are inferred. That means if you don't provide a type, TypeScript will assign
one depending on the value. See Listing 2-2.

Listing 2-2. String and Boolean types

```
//String
let myStr: string = 'Hello';
let anotherStr = 'World';
myStr = true;
anotherStr = 45;
//Boolean
let myBool: boolean = true;
let anotherBool = false;

myBool = 'true';
anotherBool = 76;
```

Inference

So, you might wonder when to assign a type and when is it better to let
TypeScript automatically assign it?

7

In most cases, you should leave it to TypeScript to assign the type. In Listing 2-3, the `salary` variable wasn't assigned a type.

Later on, you will assign a `number`, `string`, and `Boolean` type to it.

Listing 2-3. Wrong Types

```
//Inference
let salary;
salary = 12000;
salary = '12000';
salary = true;
```

Now, this is not right. When you want to assign a value later, you'll provide an explicit type.

You will now start getting type errors, as shown in Listing 2-4.

Listing 2-4. Type Errors with Inference

```
//Inference
let salary:number;
salary = 12000;
salary = '12000';
salary = true;
```

Objects

This section explains what objects are in TypeScript. In the example in Listing 2-5, an object that has two strings is given one `number` and one `Boolean` type.

If you hover your mouse over the object, it will indicate the data types.

Listing 2-5. Object with No Types

```
//Objects
const developer = {
    firstName: 'Nabendu',
    lastName: 'Biswas',
    age: 40,
    isTrainer: true
}
```

Now create a new object where you will give the type of each key (see Listing 2-6). You will get an error if you try to assign a different value to a key or to a key that doesn't exist. See Figure 2-4.

Listing 2-6. Object with Types

```
const newDeveloper: { name: string; age: number; isDev:
boolean } = {
    name: 'Mousam',
    age: 39,
    isDev: true
}

newDeveloper.name = 'Mousam Mishra';
newDeveloper.age = 'Forty';
newDeveloper.firstName = 'Mousam';
```

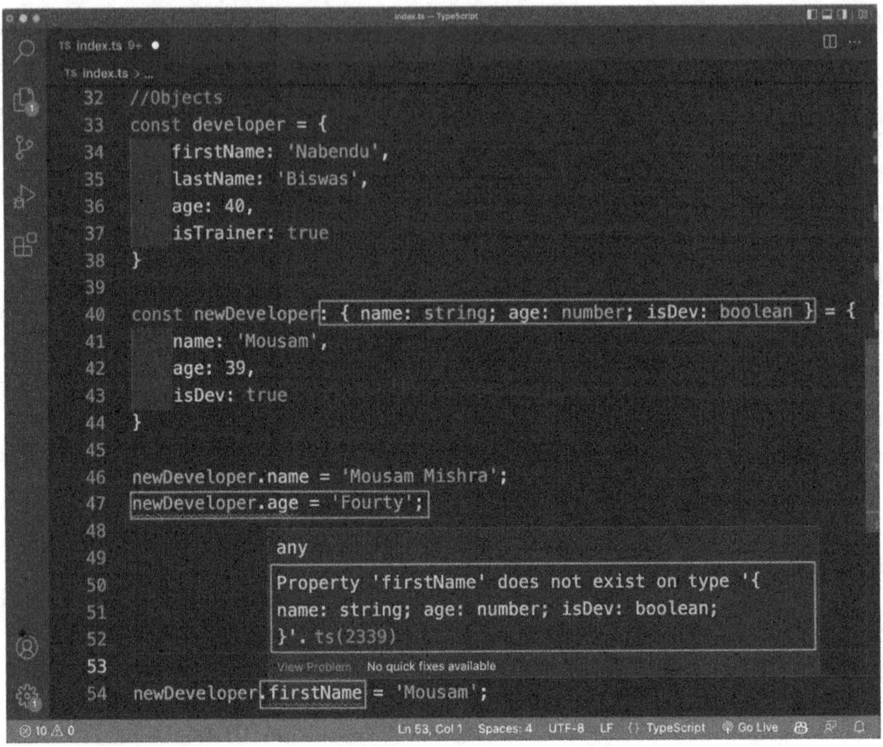

Figure 2-4. *Object errors*

Arrays

This section looks at arrays. In TypeScript, if you provide an array of strings, such as languages in the following example, you cannot push a number or Boolean type to that array.

You can also explicitly declare that you have an array of a certain type, such as declaring an array of number types. See Listing 2-7.

Listing 2-7. Arrays with Types

```
//Arrays
const languages = ['React', 'Angular', 'Vue'];

languages.push('TypeScript');
languages.push(56);
languages.push(true);

const numbers: number[] = [51, 22, 33];
numbers.push(56);
numbers.push('56');
numbers.push(true);
```

Complex Arrays

In this section, you learn to create an array of objects. You provide the type and you indicate the type of keys in the object (see Listing 2-8).

Listing 2-8. Complex Arrays with Types

```
const arrOfObj: { name: string; age: number }[] = [
    { name: 'Nabendu', age: 40 },
    { name: 'Mousam', age: 39 }
];
arrOfObj.push({ name: 'Shikha', age: 39 });
arrOfObj.push({ name: 'Hriday', age: 'Eight' });
```

If you want to write the array type, you need to use two brackets [ ] in the type inference, as shown in Listing 2-9.

Listing 2-9. More Complex Arrays with Types

```
const arrOfArrays: number[][] = [
    [11, 32, 43],
    [34, 75, 64]
];

arrOfArrays.push([21, 32, 13]);
```

Functions

This section looks at the example of functions. Suppose you need to add two numbers and create a function called addNums to do so.

If you don't provide the type, you will not get an error even if you give one string. See Listing 2-10.

Listing 2-10. Functions

```
//Functions
const addNums = (num1, num2) => {
    return num1 + num2;
}

addNums(10, 20);
addNums(10, '20');
```

You should always provide the type, as in multiNums. It is also advisable to provide the return type, as it can catch the error if you provide the wrong return type, as in modNums.

If you don't give a return type, you should provide void, as shown in printSum in Listing 2-11.

Listing 2-11. Function Types

```
const multiNums = (num1: number, num2: number) => {
    return num1 * num2;
}

multiNums(10, 20);
multiNums(10, '20');

const modNums = (num1: number, num2: number): number => {
    // return num1 % num2;
    return num1 > num2
}

modNums(10, 20);
modNums(10, '20');

const printSum = (num1: number, num2: number): void => {
    console.log(num1 + num2);
}

printSum(10, 20);
printSum(10, '20');
```

Union Types

You can also create union types, in which a variable can have multiple types. Say you have a variable called numOrStr, which can be a number or string type.

You can also have an array, which can only contain elements of the number or string type. See Listing 2-12.

Listing 2-12. Union Types

```
//Union types
let numOrStr: number | string;
numOrStr = 10;
numOrStr = 'Ten';

let arr: (number | string )[] = [10, 'Ten', true];
```

Literal Types

With literal types, you specify only the acceptable terms. For example, in the myLiteral type, Nabendu, Mousam, Shikha, and Hriday are the only acceptable values.

Listing 2-13 uses Parag and the program returns errors.

Listing 2-13. Literal Types

```
//Literal types
let myLiteral: 'Nabendu' | 'Mousam' | 'Shikha' | 'Hriday' =
'Nabendu';

myLiteral = 'Mousam';
myLiteral = 'Shikha';
myLiteral = 'Hriday';
myLiteral = 'Parag';
```

Enum Types

This section looks at enum, which is a combination of the union type and the literal type. Listing 2-14 provides a predefined type with the enum variable.

After that, you can use it in your code.

Listing 2-14. Enum Types

```
//Enum
enum Role { ADMIN, READ_ONLY, AUTHOR };

const myRole = Role.ADMIN;
const hridayRole: Role = Role.AUTHOR;
```

Optionals Type

This section looks at *optionals*. Suppose you want an age field, which should be a number.

In the example in Listing 2-15, in optionalObj, the age is declared as a number and is undefined. The problem with this approach is that you need to leave it undefined if you don't want to specify it.

In the betterOptObj example, the age is indicated with ?, which means if you provide it, it should be a number, but it is not required.

Listing 2-15. Optionals Types

```
//Optionals
let optionalObj: { name: string; age: number | undefined } = {
    name: 'Nabendu',
    age: undefined
};

let betterOptObj: { name: string; age?: number } = {
    name: 'Nabendu'
};
```

15

Interfaces and Types

This section looks at interfaces. They are a better way to provide types for different properties of an object. Listing 2-16 shows a Developer interface that includes some properties.

You can use this interface in two different variables, called person1 and person2.

Listing 2-16. Interfaces

```
//Interfaces
interface Developer {
    name: string;
    age: number;
    isDev: boolean;
}

const person1: Developer = {
    name: 'Nabendu',
    age: 40,
    isDev: true
}

const person2: Developer = {
    name: 'Mousam',
    age: 39,
    isDev: true
}
```

Types are similar to interfaces. As you can see in Listing 2-17, they are used in DeveloperType.

Interfaces can be used only in objects, whereas types can be used in strings, arrays of objects, or anything else.

Listing 2-17. Types

```
//Types
type DeveloperType = {
    name: string;
    age: number;
    isDev: boolean;
}

const person3: DeveloperType = {
    name: 'Nabendu',
    age: 40,
    isDev: true
}

type PersonName = string;
const person4: PersonName = 'Nabendu';

type CoderType = {
    name: string;
    category: 'frontend' | 'backend' | 'mobile';
    age: number;
}[];

const coder1: CoderType = [
    {   name: 'Nabendu', category: 'frontend', age: 40 },
    {   name: 'Mousam', category: 'backend', age: 39 },
]
```

Running the Code

Since the index.ts file has a lot of errors, you will add a bit of it to the main.ts file. You also need to run the tsc main.ts command to convert the code into a JavaScript file. See Listing 2-18.

Listing 2-18. Running the Code

```
//Types
type DeveloperNewType = {
    name: string;
    age: number;
    isDev: boolean;
}
const person5: DeveloperNewType = {
    name: 'Nabendu',
    age: 40,
    isDev: true
}
console.log('${person5.name} is a ${person5.isDev} Dev and is
${person5.age} years old');
```

Now, in the localhost, you can see the desired console log (see Figure 2-5).

Figure 2-5. *The console*

Summary

In this chapter, you learned about different types in TypeScript. You learned about the `number` type and then moved to `string` and `Boolean` types. After learning about object and array types, you learned about complex arrays. Then you learned about union, literal, enum, and optional types. The chapter ended by discussing interfaces.

CHAPTER 3

The TypeScript Compiler

When you run the TypeScript file every time, you are making changes to it. In this chapter, you learn about other ways to watch for and make changes.

Watch Mode

You can watch the changes in the `main.js` file by using watch mode. Then you don't have to run the file after each change. You need to run the `tsc` command with the `-w` flag, as follows:

```
1   tsc main.ts -w
```

If you then add anything to the file, it will be converted into the corresponding JavaScript file. See Listing 3-1.

Listing 3-1. New Code

```
type PersonNewName = string;
const person6: PersonNewName = 'Mousam';
console.log(`New Developer is ${person6}`);
```

You can see the new changes in the localhost (see Figure 3-1).

© Nabendu Biswas 2023

N. Biswas, *TypeScript Basics*, https://doi.org/10.1007/978-1-4842-9523-6_3

Figure 3-1. *Local changes*

Compiling an Entire Project

To compile an entire project, you have to make it a TypeScript project. You need to run the `tsc -init` command, which will create a `tsconfig.json` file in the root directory. See Figure 3-2.

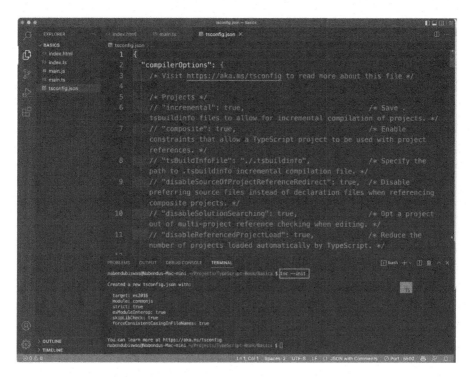

Figure 3-2. *Compiling a project*

You can then run the `tsc` command to compile all the TypeScript files. However, the `index.ts` file has a lot of errors. Figure 3-3 shows one of these errors.

Figure 3-3. *The tsc error*

You need to exclude this file by adding an `exclude` to the `tsconfig.json` file. Now, when you run the `tsc` command, you will not get an error (see Figure 3-4).

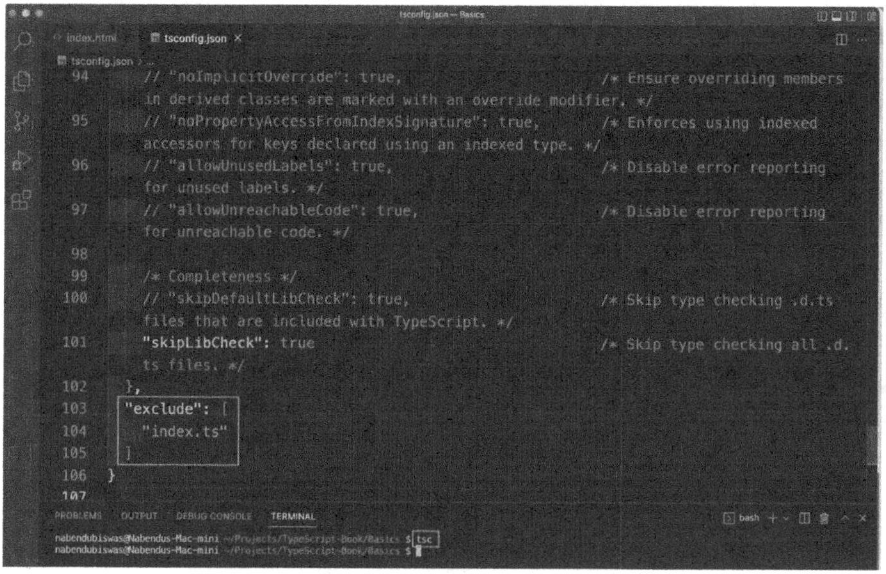

Figure 3-4. *The tsc file again, without the error*

You can also exclude all the node_modules, which are created when you use a third-party library. Sometimes they contain TypeScript code and you don't want to compile them.

Similar to using exclude, you have use include to add the mentioned files. In the example in Figure 3-5, the main.ts file is included.

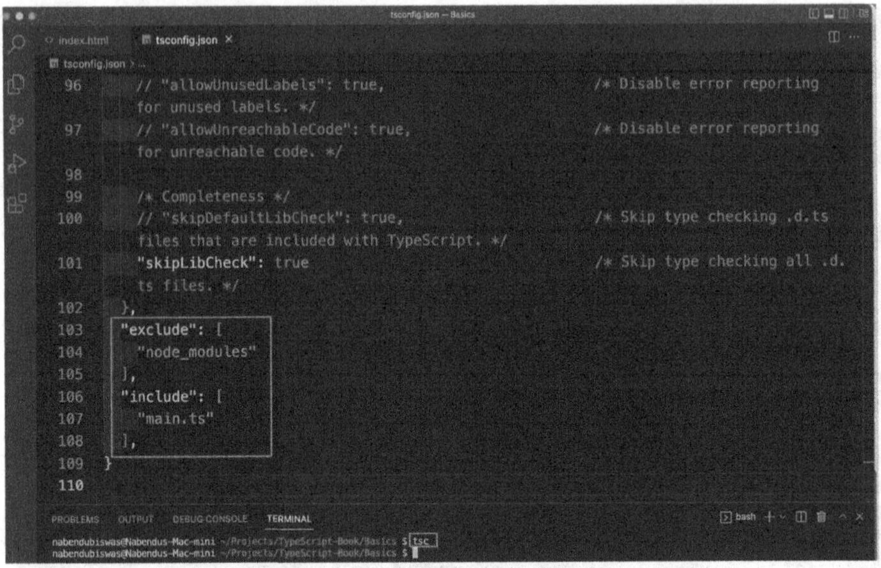

Figure 3-5. *This include adds the main.ts file*

rootDir and outDir

To organize your TypeScript project, you should keep all the TypeScript files in a `src` folder.

You have put the `index.ts` and `main.ts` files in the `src` folder. Also create a `dist` folder.

In the `tsconfig.json` file, uncomment `rootDir` and `outDir`. This is where you put the respective folders (see Figure 3-6). You also have to run the `tsc` command; it is not throwing an error.

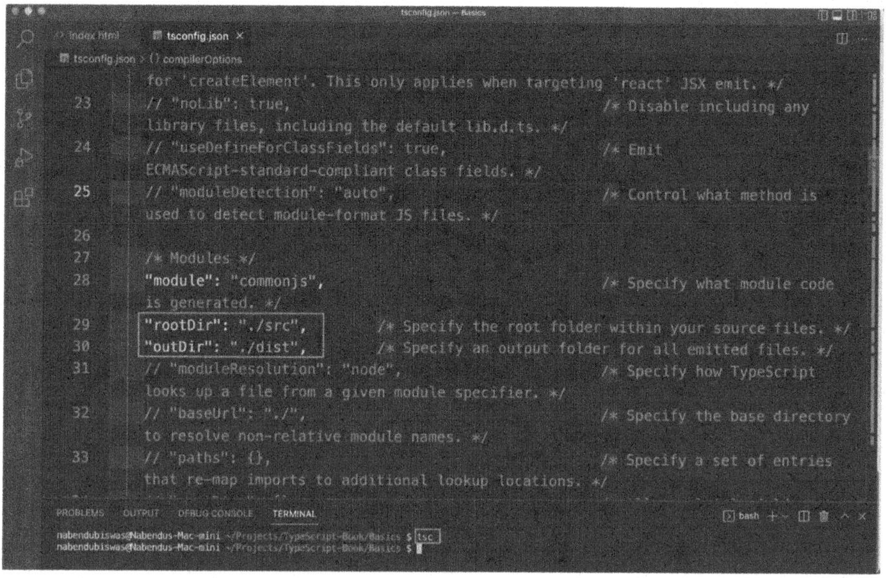

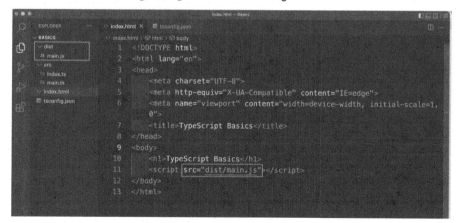

Figure 3-6. *The tsconfig.json file*

You can now see the `main.js` file in the `dist` folder (see Figure 3-7).
You also need to change the path of the `main.js` file in the `index.html` file.

Figure 3-7. *The index.html file*

Summary

In this chapter, you learned to configure your TypeScript projects properly.

27

CHAPTER 4

Classes and Interfaces

This chapter covers classes and interfaces. In order to follow along, you should have basic knowledge of ES6 classes.

The Basics about Classes

TypeScript classes have some special features. TypeScript classes can have public and private variables, like OOP languages such as Java and C++ do.

Listing 4-1 shows a class called CreateRoom. It has a public variable called room and a private family array.

You can add values to the family array only by using the addFamilyMember function and you can get values using the showFamily function.

Listing 4-1. Classes

```
//Classes
class CreateRoom{
    public room: string;
    private family: string[] = [];
    constructor(name: string){
        this.room = '${name}s room'
    }
```

```
    addFamilyMember(member: string){
        this.family.push(member);
    }
    showFamily(){
        console.log(this.family);
    }
    cleanRoom(soap: string){
        console.log('Cleaning ${this.room} with ${soap}');
    }
}

const nabendu = new CreateRoom('Nabendu');
const shikha = new CreateRoom('Shikha');
const hriday = new CreateRoom('Hriday');
const mousam = new CreateRoom('Mousam');
nabendu.family;
nabendu.addFamilyMember('Nabendu');
shikha.addFamilyMember('Shikha');
hriday.addFamilyMember('Hriday');
mousam.cleanRoom('Lizol');
```

You can also use read-only variables in TypeScript. In Listing 4-2, dobShikha is a read-only variable. You can access it from outside of the class, but you cannot update it.

You can make a variable private and read-only both (like dobHriday). That way, you cannot access the variable from the outside.

Listing 4-2. Private and Read-Only Variables

```
//Classes
class CreateRoom{
    public room: string;
    private family: string[] = [];
    readonly dobShikha: string = '1982-12-12';
```

```
    private readonly dobHriday: string = '2013-12-12';
    constructor(name: string){
        this.room = '${name}s room'
    }
    ...
}

const nabendu = new CreateRoom('Nabendu');
const shikha = new CreateRoom('Shikha');
const hriday = new CreateRoom('Hriday');
const mousam = new CreateRoom('Mousam');
shikha.dobShikha;
shikha.dobShikha = '1982-11-12';
hriday.dobHriday;
...
...
```

You can clean up a TypeScript class by using the constructor.
In Listing 4-3, room in the constructor has been removed and is now public.

Listing 4-3. Updating the Constructor

```
class CreateRoom{
    private family: string[] = [];
    readonly dobShikha: string = '1982-12-12';
    private readonly dobHriday: string = '2013-12-12';
    constructor(public room: string){
    }
    ...
    ...
    cleanRoom(soap: string){
        console.log('Cleaning ${this.room} with ${soap}');
    }
}
```

Listing 4-4 creates a new file called classDemo.ts in the src folder. You can utilize the class from the earlier part. There are no errors in this file.

Listing 4-4. New Class

```
//Classes
class Room{
    private family: string[] = [];
    readonly dobShikha: string = '1982-12-12';
    private readonly dobHriday: string = '2013-12-12';
    constructor(public room: string){
    }

    addFamilyMember(member: string){
        this.family.push(member);
    }
    showFamily(){
        console.log(this.family);
    }
    cleanRoom(soap: string){
        console.log('Cleaning ${this.room} with ${soap}');
    }
}

const nab = new Room('Nabendu');
const shi = new Room('Shikha');
const hri = new Room('Hriday');
const mou = new Room('Mousam');
nab.dobShikha;
nab.addFamilyMember('Nabendu');
nab.addFamilyMember('Shikha');
nab.addFamilyMember('Hriday');
nab.cleanRoom('Lizol');
nab.showFamily();
```

You also need to add this new file to `tsconfig.json` in the `include` array. After that, run the `tsc` command from an integrated terminal. See Figure 4-1.

Figure 4-1. *The tsconfig.json file*

Now, you will add the JavaScript file to `index.html`. You can see the new output in the console for the localhost. See Figure 4-2.

Figure 4-2. *The index.html file*

Advanced Classes

This section covers advanced topics related to classes. It starts with *inheritance*.

Using inheritance, you can inherit from a base class. Say you created a new class called OyoRoom in the classDemo.ts file. You have extended it from room using the extends keyword.

In the constructor, you have to take the earlier room variable and use super() to call it. You can also add a new variable to the constructor. Here, you are adding the roomRent variable. This utilizes the shortcut discussed earlier.

Next, add two new functions to the OyoRoom class—to update the rent and to show the rent.

Lastly, you create a new object called shekar and initialize it with values. This example uses showRoomRent and changeRoomRent from this class. It also uses cleanRoom from the parent class of Room. See Listing 4-5.

Listing 4-5. Extending Classes

```
class OyoRoom extends Room{
    constructor(room: string, private roomRent: number){
        super(room);
    }

    changeRoomRent(rent: number){
        this.roomRent = rent;
    }

    showRoomRent(){
        console.log('${this.room}'s room rent is ${this.
        roomRent}');
    }
}
```

```
const shekar = new OyoRoom('Shekar', 1000);
shekar.showRoomRent();
shekar.changeRoomRent(2000);
shekar.showRoomRent();
shekar.cleanRoom('Phenyl');
```

Now, after running the tsc command from the terminal, you can see the updated console log in the localhost (see Figure 4-3).

TypeScript Basics

Figure 4-3. *The localhost shows the updated console log*

Override the function of addFamilyMember in the OyoRoom class. The family array is private, so you should change it to protected. Now, any inherited class can access it. See Listing 4-6.

Listing 4-6. Adding a Protected Class

```
//Classes
class Room{
    protected family: string[] = [];
```

```
    readonly dobShikha: string = '1982-12-12';
    private readonly dobHriday: string = '2013-12-12';
    constructor(public room: string){
    }
    ...
    ...
}

class OyoRoom extends Room{
    constructor(room: string, private roomRent: number){
        super(room);
    }

    addFamilyMember(member: string){
        if(member === 'Kapil')
            return
        this.family.push(member);
    }
    ...
    ...
}
```

Next, add the shobha and kapil objects to OyoRoom. You can also add the members using addFamilyMember and run showFamily. See Listing 4-7.

Listing 4-7. Adding Objects

```
const shekar = new OyoRoom('Shekar', 1000);
const shobha = new OyoRoom('Shobha', 1000);
const kapil = new OyoRoom('Shobha', 1000);
shekar.addFamilyMember('Shekar');
shekar.addFamilyMember('Shobha');
shekar.addFamilyMember('Kapil');
```

```
shekar.showFamily();
shekar.showRoomRent();
shekar.changeRoomRent(2000);
shekar.showRoomRent();
shekar.cleanRoom('Phenyl');
```

Now, in the localhost, you can see that Shekar and Shobha were added. Kapil was not added, as you have the logic for it in addFamilyMember, in the OyoRoom class. See Figure 4-4.

Figure 4-4. *The localhost*

You can access private variables in a class, through setters and getters. You now have a Report array in OyoRoom, which is private.

You can access it through a function called allReports with the get keyword. You can then add a new report using the newReport function, which uses the set keyword.

Then you can add a new report to the newReport function by assigning a value to it. You also get all the reports by calling allReports. But notice that this doesn't use () in allReports.

37

Listing 4-8. The Getter and Setter

```
class OyoRoom extends Room{
    private reports: string[] = [];

    get allReports(){
        return this.reports;
    }

    set newReport(report: string){
        this.reports.push(report);
    }

    ...
    ...
}

const shekar = new OyoRoom('Shekar', 1000);
const shobha = new OyoRoom('Shobha', 1000);
const kapil = new OyoRoom('Shobha', 1000);
shekar.newReport = 'Year End Report';
console.log(shekar.allReports);
```

The new Report array can be seen in the localhost, as shown in Figure 4-5.

Figure 4-5. *The new Report array*

Here, you learn about *static* methods and properties. They are used to create utility methods or properties and can be accessed without creating an object.

In the OyoRoom class, create a static variable called currentYear. You also need to create a static function called createRoom.

Then create a variable called rohit, through which you call the createRoom function directly. You do not create an object. This example also calls the currentYear variable directly. See Listing 4-9.

Listing 4-9. Static Variables and Functions

```
class OyoRoom extends Room{
    private reports: string[] = [];
    static currentYear = 2022;

    get allReports(){
        return this.reports;
    }

    set newReport(report: string){
        this.reports.push(report);
    }

    constructor(room: string, private roomRent: number){
        super(room);
    }

    static createRoom(room: string){
        return { room: room };
    }
    ...
    ...
}
```

```
const rohit = OyoRoom.createRoom('Rohit');
console.log(rohit);
console.log(OyoRoom.currentYear);
const shekar = new OyoRoom('Shekar', 1000);
```

The new static variables can now be seen in the localhost, as shown in Figure 4-6.

Figure 4-6. *Static variables*

The next thing you learn about is *abstract* classes. You are going to learn how to make the base class of Room abstract. You also create the cleanRoom function as abstract and remove all the statements from it.

When you make a function abstract, it is the responsibility of the inherited class to implement it. Listing 4-10 implements the cleanRoom method in OyoRoom.

Listing 4-10. An Abstract Class

```
//Classes
abstract class Room{
    protected family: string[] = [];
    readonly dobShikha: string = '1982-12-12';
```

```
    private readonly dobHriday: string = '2013-12-12';
    constructor(public room: string){
    }

    addFamilyMember(member: string){
        this.family.push(member);
    }
    showFamily(){
        console.log(this.family);
    }

    abstract cleanRoom(soap: string): void;
}
class OyoRoom extends Room{
    private reports: string[] = [];
    static currentYear = 2022;

    cleanRoom(soap: string){
        console.log('${this.room}'s Oyo Room cleaned with
        ${soap}');
    }

    get allReports(){
        return this.reports;
    }
    ...
    ...
}
```

The abstract class cannot have its object. You would get an error if you created an instance of the Room class, as shown in Figure 4-7.

```
constructor Room(room: string): Room
Cannot create an instance of an abstract class. ts(2511)
View Problem    No quick fixes available

68  const nab = new Room('Nabendu');
69  const shi = new Room('Shikha');
70  const hri = new Room('Hriday');
71  const mou = new Room('Mousam');
72  nab.dobShikha;
73  nab.addFamilyMember('Nabendu');
74  nab.addFamilyMember('Shikha');
75  nab.addFamilyMember('Hriday');
76  mou.cleanRoom('Lizol');
77  nab.showFamily();
```

Figure 4-7. *The error*

If you comment this out, everything will work fine, as shown in
Figure 4-8.

Figure 4-8. *Commented out errors*

The last thing about classes that you learn is *private constructors*. They
are used to implement the *singleton* pattern. With this pattern, you can
have only one instance of any class. You cannot create multiple objects of a
class in such a scenario.

Consider a new class called TreboHotel in which the constructor is private. You create instances of it using the getInstance method from inside the class.

Next, you create an object called vijay by calling this method. See Listing 4-11.

Listing 4-11. A Singleton Pattern

```
class TreboHotel extends Room{
    private static instance: TreboHotel;
    private constructor(room: string, private roomRent:
    number){
        super(room);
    }

    static getInstance(){
        if(!TreboHotel.instance){
            TreboHotel.instance = new TreboHotel('Trebo', 1000);
        }
        return TreboHotel.instance;
    }

    cleanRoom(soap: string){
        console.log('${this.room}'s Trebo Room cleaned with
        ${soap}');
    }
}

const vijay = TreboHotel.getInstance();
console.log(vijay);
```

You can now see the new object in the localhost, as shown in Figure 4-9.

Figure 4-9. *The Singleton object*

Interface Basics

You looked at interfaces briefly in Chapter 2, where you used them to create types for objects. You can use interfaces in other situations as well.

This example works with a new file called `interfaceDemo.ts`. You first need to import the file in the `index.html` file. See Listing 4-12.

Listing 4-12. Interface Addition

```
<body>
    <h1>TypeScript Basics</h1>
    <script src="dist/main.js"></script>
    <script src="dist/classDemo.js"></script>
    <script src="dist/interfaceDemo.js"></script>
</body>
```

Next, add it to the `tsconfig.json` file, as shown in Listing 4-13.

Listing 4-13. Interface Addition

```
"include": [
  "src/main.ts",
  "src/classDemo.ts",
  "src/interfaceDemo.ts"
]
```

Now, you create an `interfaceDemo.ts` file in the `src` folder. This example creates an interface called `Greeting`, through which you are given a variable name and a function called `greet`.

Next, you create a class called `Person`, which implements `Greeting`. This example uses both the name and the greet function.

Finally, you create a developer object and call the greet function from it, as shown in Listing 4-14.

Listing 4-14. The interfaceDemo.ts File

```
interface Greeting {
    name: string;
    greet(sentence: string): void;
}

class Person implements Greeting {
    constructor(public name: string) {}

    greet(sentence: string): void {
        console.log('${sentence} ${this.name}');
    }
}

let developer: Greeting = new Person('Kapil');
developer.greet('Hello from');
```

You'll see the new console log in the localhost, as shown in Figure 4-10.

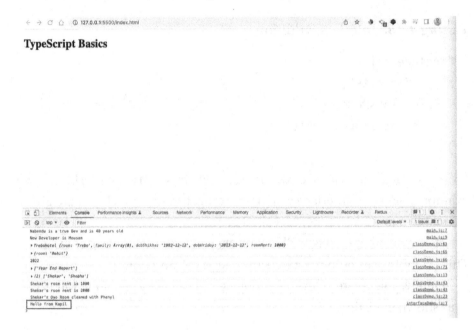

Figure 4-10. *Interface console*

You can also make a property read-only. If you make a name read-only, you won't be able to set it directly. Figure 4-11 shows the error.

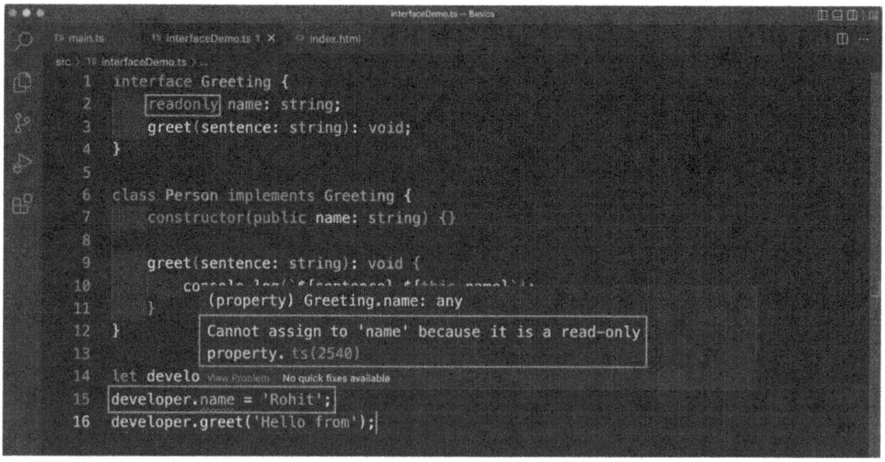

Figure 4-11. *A read-only error*

Next, you see how to divide the Greeting interface. You move the name variable to another interface, called Naming. Then you extend it in the Greeting interface. See Listing 4-15.

Listing 4-15. Read-Only in a File

```
interface Naming{
    readonly name: string;
}

interface Greeting extends Naming {
    greet(sentence: string): void;
}

class Person implements Greeting {
    ...
    ...
}
```

47

```
let developer: Greeting = new Person('Kapil');
// developer.name = 'Rohit';
developer.greet('Hello from');
```

You can also use optional parameters in interfaces. In the Naming interface for, example, there is an optional parameter called nickName. Notice that you have to use ? to make it optional.

You don't have to use it and you are not using it in the Person class. However, the new Dog class uses the nickName. See Listing 4-16.

Listing 4-16. Optional Parameter in the Interface

```
interface Naming{
    readonly name: string;
    nickName?: string;
}

interface Greeting extends Naming {
    greet(sentence: string): void;
}

class Person implements Greeting {

    ...

    ...

}

class Dog implements Greeting {
    nickName: string = "Doggy";
    constructor(public name: string) {}
    greet(sentence: string): void {
        console.log('${sentence} ${this.name}');
    }
}
```

```
let dog: Greeting = new Dog("Rocket");
console.log(dog.nickName);
dog.greet("Woof from");
```

You can now see the new console log in the localhost, as shown in Figure 4-12.

Figure 4-12. *Optional parameter in the interface*

Summary

In this chapter, you learned everything about classes. Classes were introduced with ES6 in JavaScript, but with TypeScript, many advanced features were added to them.

You learned about protected variables, static functions, abstract classes, and singleton patterns in classes. You also learned about interfaces in detail.

CHAPTER 5

Advanced Types

In this chapter, you learn about advanced types. These are special types that can be used in TypeScript. They include intersection types, type guards and discriminated unions, type casting, index properties, function overloading, and nullish coalescing.

Initial Setup

You will be using a new file in the project called advancedDemo.ts. Create this file in the src folder. You only need to show the output of it, so keep the output and remove everything else in the index.html file, as shown in Listing 5-1.

Listing 5-1. Adding an Advanced File

```
<body>
    <h1>TypeScript Basics</h1>
    <script src="dist/advancedDemo.js"></script>
</body>
```

Next, you include this in the tsconfig.json file and start the tsc in watch mode by running tsc -w. See Listing 5-2.

© Nabendu Biswas 2023
N. Biswas, *TypeScript Basics*, https://doi.org/10.1007/978-1-4842-9523-6_5

Listing 5-2. Adding the File to tsconfig.json

```
"exclude": [
  "node_modules"
],
"include": [
  "src/advancedDemo.ts"
]
```

Intersection Types

You can combine two types using the & operator. The `advancedDemo.ts` file has two types—`ITadmin` and `Employee`.

You can combine them to form a new `AdminEmployee` type with the & operator. Next, create an admin employee called `emp1` with all required fields and log it in the console. See Listing 5-3.

Listing 5-3. Creating the advancedDemo.ts File

```
//Intersection Types
type ITadmin = {
    access: string[];
}

type Employee = {
    name: string;
    startDate: Date;
    skills: string[];
}

type AdminEmployee = Employee & ITadmin;

const emp1: AdminEmployee = {
    name: 'John',
```

```
    startDate: new Date(),
    skills: ['Cisco', 'Python', 'Perl'],
    access: ['admin', 'user']
}
```

```
console.log(emp1);
```

As shown in Figure 5-1, you'll get emp1 in the console of the localhost.

Figure 5-1. *TypeScript console*

Type Guards and Discriminated Unions

You can use Type with the OR operator(|). In the example in Listing 5-4, the two interfaces (Human and Horse) have different properties.

If you create a type of mammal that can be either Human or Horse, you use an OR operator.

The moveMammal functions checks whether walkingSpeed or runningSpeed was passed. This process uses Type Guards and the if statement to check whether walkingSpeed is in mammal. It shows a console log according to the results. Otherwise, it shows the console logs for Horse.

53

Without the Type Guards, you won't be able to use the `moveMammal` function. See Listing 5-4.

Listing 5-4. Type Guards

```
interface Human {
    walkingSpeed: number;
}

interface Horse {
    runningSpeed: number;
}

type Mammal = Human | Horse;

function moveMammal(mammal: Mammal) {
    if('walkingSpeed' in mammal){
        console.log('Human is moving at ${mammal.
        walkingSpeed} km/h');
    } else {
        console.log('Horse is moving at ${mammal.
        runningSpeed} km/h');
    }
}

moveMammal({ walkingSpeed: 10 });
moveMammal({ runningSpeed: 40 });
```

In the console of the localhost, you'll get the correct log for Human and Horse, as shown in Figure 5-2.

TypeScript Basics

Figure 5-2. *Console for Type Guards*

There is a different pattern, called *discriminated unions,* that can achieve this same effect. This pattern adds a type. Now, inside the moveMammal function, you have a switch case by type. It shows the different console logs.

Note that in the call to the moveMammal function, you have to send a type. See Listing 5-5.

Listing 5-5. Discriminated Unions

```
interface Human {
    type: 'human';
    walkingSpeed: number;
}

interface Horse {
    type: 'horse';
    runningSpeed: number;
}
```

```
type Mammal = Human | Horse;

function moveMammal(mammal: Mammal) {
    switch(mammal.type) {
        case 'human':
            console.log('Human is moving at ${mammal.
            walkingSpeed} km/h');
            break;
        case 'horse':
            console.log('Horse is moving at ${mammal.
            runningSpeed} km/h');
            break;
    }
}

moveMammal({ type:'human', walkingSpeed: 10 });
moveMammal({ type:'horse', runningSpeed: 40 });
```

Type Casting

When you work with DOM elements, it is very important for TypeScript to know the element's type. TypeScript doesn't go through the HTML file, so it is important to provide the correct type.

Listing 5-6 uses a new input type in index.html with the input-user ID.

Listing 5-6. Adding Type Casting

```
<body>
    <h1>TypeScript Basics</h1>
    <input type="text" id="input-user">
    <script src="dist/advancedDemo.js"></script>
</body>
```

Next in the TypeScript file, you select it with the usual `getElementById`. But there is also an ! after it. It tells the expression before it that it will never be null. After that, you tell TypeScript with the as keyword that it is an `HTMLInputElement`.

After that, you have the usual event listener code. It also tells TypeScript that it is optional by using ?. Also inside the event listener, you have to indicate that the target is `HTMLInputElement`. See Listing 5-7.

Listing 5-7. Type Casting

```
//Type Casting
const inputUser = document.getElementById('input-user')! as
HTMLInputElement;

inputUser?.addEventListener('input', (event) => {
    const target = event.target as HTMLInputElement;
    console.log(target.value);
});
```

Now, you will get the correct result in the localhost, as shown in Figure 5-3.

Figure 5-3. *Type casting is working*

Index Properties

You can provide index properties in interfaces as well, which means that you can indicate the type of key and value an object is expecting.

In the example in Listing 5-8, you have an interface called ErrorMessages, which expects key and value to be strings.

Now, when creating an object, you give the keys and values as strings.

Listing 5-8. Index Properties

```
//Index Properties
interface ErrorMessages {
    [key: string]: string;
}
```

```
const errorMessages: ErrorMessages = {
    name: 'Name is required',
    email: 'Email is required',
    password: 'Password is required'
}
```

Function Overloading

In the example in Listing 5-9, the addElements function can add two numbers or two strings. It can also add a string and a number. This example uses the StrOrNum type, which means it can take a string or number.

You can pass different combinations to it. But when you try a string method like split(), TypeScript will throw an error because it doesn't know the result type.

Listing 5-9. Function Overloading Problem

```
//Function Overloading
type StrOrNum = string | number;

function addElements(a: StrOrNum, b: StrOrNum){
    if(typeof a === 'string' || typeof b === 'string') {
        return a.toString() + b.toString();
    }
    return a + b;
}

const result = addElements(1, 2);
const result2 = addElements('Nabendu', ' Biswas');
const result3 = addElements('Nabendu ', 2);
result2.split('');
```

To solve this issue, you have to specify the different type of function calls that are acceptable before the actual function call. See Listing 5-10.

Listing 5-10. Function Overloading

```
//Function Overloading
type StrOrNum = string | number;

function addElements(a: number, b: number): number;
function addElements(a: string, b: string): string;
function addElements(a: string, b: number): string;
function addElements(a: number, b: string): string;
function addElements(a: StrOrNum, b: StrOrNum){
    if(typeof a === 'string' || typeof b === 'string') {
        return a.toString() + b.toString();
    }
    return a + b;
}

const result = addElements(1, 2);
const result2 = addElements('Nabendu', ' Biswas');
const result3 = addElements('Nabendu ', 2);
console.log(result);
console.log(result2);
console.log(result3);
console.log(result2.split(''));
```

You will get the desired output in the localhost, as shown in Figure 5-4.

Figure 5-4. *Function overloading console*

Nullish Coalescing

You can use *nullish coalescing* to require better behavior of null and undefined values.

The example in Listing 5-11 uses the OR (||) operator. For an empty string, you will get Default, because empty strings are considered falsy values in JavaScript.

If you use ?? in place of ||, it will consider only null and undefined as default values.

Listing 5-11. Nullish Coalescing

```
//Nullish Coalescing
const theInput = '';
const storedInput = theInput || 'Default';
console.log(storedInput);
```

```
const theInput2 = '';
const storedInput2 = theInput2 ?? 'Default 2';
console.log(storedInput2);

const theInput3 = null;
const storedInput3 = theInput3 ?? 'Default 3';
console.log(storedInput3);
```

You get the correct output in the localhost, as shown in Figure 5-5.

Figure 5-5. *Nullish coalescing in the console*

Summary

In this chapter, you learned everything about advanced types in TypeScript. These advanced types include intersection types, function overloading, and others. In the next chapter, you learn about generics and decorators.

CHAPTER 6

Generics and Decorators

In this chapter, you learn about the advanced topics of generics and decorators. You also learn about the Array and Promise types, generic functions, type constraints, generic classes, and different decorators, including decorator factories.

Initial Setup

Create a file for this project called genericsDemo.ts in the src folder. To just show the output of it, Listing 6-1 removes everything else from the index.html file.

Listing 6-1. Initial Setup

```html
<body>
    <h1>TypeScript Basics</h1>
    <input type="text" id="input-user">
    <script src="dist/genericsDemo.js"></script>
</body>
```

Listing 6-2 shows the script added to the tsconfig.json file. Next, start the tsc in watch mode by running tsc -w.

Listing 6-2. Adding the tsconfig.json File

```
"include": [
  "src/genericsDemo.ts"
]
```

Array and Promise Types

For the Array and Promise generic types, you have to provide the return value in <> brackets.

The example in Listing 6-3 declares an array called occupation. It returns a string value. Next, the Promise type also returns a string value.

The resolve and reject functions have to send back a string. The then block uses the string method called split. TypeScript won't produce an error, because you are getting a string back.

Listing 6-3. Array and Promise Types

```
//Array Type
const occupation: Array<string> = [];

//Promise type
const promise: Promise<string> = new Promise((resolve,
reject) => {
    setTimeout(() => {
        let num = Math.random();
        num > 0.5 ? resolve('It is Success') : reject('It
        is Fail');
    }, 2000);
})

promise
    .then(data => console.log(data.split('')))
    .catch(err => console.log(err));
```

Figure 6-1 shows the split data, indicating a successful run.

Figure 6-1. *Successful data*

Generic Functions

You can also create *generic function types.* Suppose you have a
mergeObject function that merges two objects.

The program calls the function with two objects (name and age) and
stores the objects in a merged variable. However, you cannot access the
name and age properties, because TypeScript has very little information
about those objects. See Listing 6-4.

Listing 6-4. Generic Function Problem

```
//Generic Function
function mergeObject(obj1: object, obj2: object) {
    return { ...obj1, ...obj2 };
}
```

```
const merged = mergeObject({ name: 'John' }, { age: 30 });
merged.name;
merged.age;
```

You can solve this issue by using a generic type for the function. Inside the <> brackets, you provide two capital letters. Now, when you hover the mouse over the function, you can see that TypeScript now knows that it is getting two variables and returns the intersection of them. See Listing 6-5.

Listing 6-5. Generic Function Resolved

```
//Generic Function
function mergeObject<T , U>(obj1: T, obj2: U) {
    return { ...obj1, ...obj2 };
}

const merged = mergeObject({ name: 'John' }, { age: 30 });
merged.name;
merged.age;
```

Type Constraints

There is an issue with the generic function in Listing 6-5. You could also pass something other than an object, like a number. See Listing 6-6.

Listing 6-6. Generic Function Issue

```
//Generic Function
function mergeObject<T , U>(obj1: T, obj2: U) {
    return { ...obj1, ...obj2 };
}

const merged = mergeObject({ name: 'John' }, 30);
console.log(merged);
```

The problem is that TypeScript will not throw an error, but will print the first object without merging it in the localhost (see Figure 6-2).

Figure 6-2. *The problem*

To solve this issue, you have to use the extends keyword and specify that they are objects. Now, the number 30 throws an error in the editor. See Listing 6-7.

Listing 6-7. Generic Function Solution

```
function mergeObject<T extends object, U extends object>
(obj1: T, obj2: U) {
    return { ...obj1, ...obj2 };
}

const merged = mergeObject({ name: 'John' }, 30);
console.log(merged);
```

Generic Classes

You can also have generic types in classes. In these cases, it is better to use the extends keyword to specify the data types that are allowed.

For example, in the StoreData class, the string and number types are allowed. The removeData function is inside this class, so if you pass a JavaScript object to the instance, it will cause an error. See Listing 6-8.

Listing 6-8. Generic Classes

```
//Generic Classes
class StoreData<T extends string | number>{
    constructor(public data: T[]) { }

    removeData(item: T) {
        this.data.splice(this.data.indexOf(item), 1);
    }

    getData() {
        return this.data;
    }
}

const stringData = new StoreData<string>(['John', 'Doe',
'Smith']);
const numberData = new StoreData<number>([21, 12, 31]);
stringData.removeData('John');
console.log(stringData.getData());
console.log(numberData.getData());
```

In the localhost, you get the correct data, as shown in Figure 6-3.

Figure 6-3. *The solution*

Generic Utilities

TypeScript also has some generic utility types and one of them is Readonly. In the example in Listing 6-9, the family variable is marked as a Readonly type, and it contains a string of arrays.

That means you cannot push into the family array or pop from it.

Listing 6-9. Generic Utility

```
//Generic Utility
const family: Readonly<string[]> = ['Nabendu', 'Shikha',
'Hriday'];
family.push('Raj');
family.pop();
```

Decorators Setup

Decorators are experimental features and are part of the next generation of JavaScript. They are used heavily in JavaScript frameworks like Angular.

For this project, create a new file called decoratorsDemo.ts in the src folder. Listing 6-10 shows only the output, with everything else in the index.html file removed.

69

Listing 6-10. Adding Decorators

```
<body>
    <h1>TypeScript Basics</h1>
    <input type="text" id="input-user">
    <script src="dist/decoratorsDemo.js"></script>
</body>
```

Since decorators are experimental features, you need to enable them through the tsconfig.json file. Make sure the target is set to es2016 and experimentalDecorators is true. See Figure 6-4.

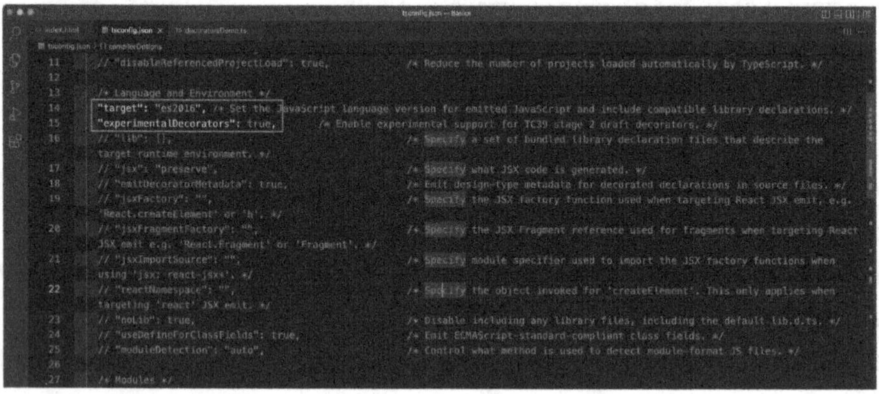

Figure 6-4. *The tsconfig.json file*

Include this file in the tsconfig.json file, as shown in Listing 6-11. Start the tsc in watch mode by running tsc -w.

Listing 6-11. Adding Decorators

```
"exclude": [
  "node_modules"
],
"include": [
  "src/decoratorsDemo.ts"
]
```

Simple Decorators

The example in Listing 6-12 starts with a simple Car class in the decoratorsDemo.ts file. The name property is inside the Car class and a constructor shows it when you create an object.

Listing 6-12. The Car Class

```
class Car{
    name = 'Tata Nexon';
    constructor(){
        console.log('Car ${this.name} created');
    }
}
const car1 = new Car();
console.log(car1)
```

A *decorator* is a function and it is applied to something, like a class. The function called Helper in Listing 6-13 is passed a parameter called constructor. The type is Function, because classes are constructor functions. In this example, you are "console-logging" the name and the constructor. Then, you add it before the class with the @ operator.

Listing 6-13. Decorator Functions

```
function Helper(constructor: Function) {
    console.log('Showing constructor: ${constructor.name}');
    console.log(constructor);
}

@Helper
class Car{
    name = 'Tata Nexon';
```

```
    constructor(){
        console.log('Car ${this.name} created');
    }
}

const car1 = new Car();
console.log(car1)
```

In the output in the localhost shown in Figure 6-5, you can see the decorator logs before the logs from the creation of the object. This happens because decorators run when the class is defined and not when it is instantiated.

Figure 6-5. *The decorator logs*

Decorator Factories

The previous function can be converted to a *decorator factory* by returning the constructor function. The benefit of doing that is that you can pass a generic string to the function. See Listing 6-14.

Listing 6-14. Decorator Factory

```
function Helper(genericString: string) {
    return function(constructor: Function) {
        console.log(genericString);
        console.log(constructor);
    }
}
@Helper('Showing constructor:')
class Car{
    name = 'Tata Nexon';
    constructor(){
        console.log('Car ${this.name} created');
    }
}

const car1 = new Car();
console.log(car1)
```

Now, in the localhost, you can see the generic log (see Figure 6-6).

Figure 6-6. *The decorator factory*

Useful Decorators

The JavaScript framework of Angular is completed based on decorators. In this section, you create a decorator similar to those found in Angular and show the HTML content.

To do this, first add an empty div with an ID of app to the index.html file, as shown in Listing 6-15.

Listing 6-15. Adding an ID

```
<body>
    <h1>TypeScript Basics</h1>
    <input type="text" id="input-user">
    <div id="app"></div>
    <script src="dist/decoratorsDemo.js"></script>
</body>
```

Next, in the decoratorsDemo.ts file, create a new function called AngularTemplate, which takes two parameters—template and hookId. Inside this, return the function, but add an underscore(_). This tells TypeScript that you know you need an argument, but you don't actually need it.

Inside the function, you first get the HTML element by using getElementById. Next, make the innerHTML equal to the template.

Through the decorator, you pass the text formatted as an <h4>, as well as the app. See Listing 6-16.

Listing 6-16. Angular Template

```
function AngularTemplate(template: string, hookId: string) {
    return function (_: any) {
        const hookEl = document.getElementById(hookId);
```

```
        if (hookEl) {
            hookEl.innerHTML = template;
        }
    }
}

// @Helper('Showing constructor:')
@AngularTemplate('<h4>This is an Angular like Template code
</h4>', 'app')
class Car{
    name = 'Tata Nexon';
    constructor(){
        console.log('Car ${this.name} created');
    }
}
```

Now, the empty div shows the text in the localhost because of the decorator, as shown in Figure 6-7.

Figure 6-7. *Angular template*

Property Decorators

You can also add decorators to various parts of a class. For example, in the Employee class in Listing 6-17, a decorator is added to the title variable.

You set the fullName and getNameWithTitle functions and the parameter of the id function.

Listing 6-17. The Employee Class

```
class Employee {
    @Log
    title: string;
    private _fullName: string;

    @Log2
    set fullName(name: string) {
        this._fullName = name;
    }

    constructor(title: string, name: string) {
        this.title = title;
        this._fullName = name;
    }

    @Log3
    getNameWithTitle(@Log4 id: number) {
        return 'Employee - ${id}, Title - ${this.title},
        Name - ${this._fullName}';
    }
}
```

Next, you need to write the code for the decorators. In Listing 6-18, you can access different things, like target, name, and descriptor.

Listing 6-18. Property Decorators

```
//Property Decorators
function Log(target: any, propertyName: string | Symbol) {
    console.log('Property decorator!');
    console.log(target, propertyName);
}

function Log2(target: any, name: string, descriptor:
PropertyDescriptor) {
    console.log('Accessor decorator!');
    console.log(target);
    console.log(name);
    console.log(descriptor);
}

function Log3( target: any, name: string | Symbol, descriptor:
PropertyDescriptor) {
    console.log('Method decorator!');
    console.log(target);
    console.log(name);
    console.log(descriptor);
}

function Log4(target: any, name: string | Symbol, position:
number) {
    console.log('Parameter decorator!');
    console.log(target);
    console.log(name);
    console.log(position);
}
```

Now, in the console log shown in Figure 6-8, you can see all the details of the various decorators.

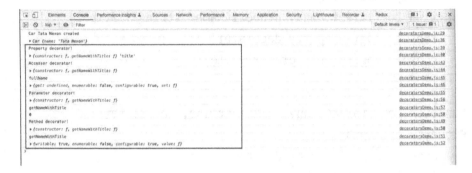

Figure 6-8. *Property decorators*

You can find the code for Chapters 1 through 6 on GitHub at `https://github.com/nabendu82/Basics-TypeScript`.

Summary

In this chapter, you learned about the advanced topics of generics and decorators. You learned about generic functions, type constraints, generic classes, and different decorators, including decorator factories. In the next chapter, you will create your first project—a to-do list.

CHAPTER 7

Creating a To-do List Project with TypeScript

With all the foundational learnings under your belt, you can now start building projects. This first project is a to-do list, which you will build using TypeScript (see Figure 7-6 for the final result).

Initial Setup

Production projects generally require build tools, as they help install dependencies and minification. In this example, you will use a build tool called snowpack to create your project.

A build tool is required for the production Vanilla TypeScript project, because you can use different third-party node modules in it.

© Nabendu Biswas 2023
N. Biswas, *TypeScript Basics*, https://doi.org/10.1007/978-1-4842-9523-6_7

Use this command to create a TypeScript project with snowpack
(see Figure 7-1):

```
1    npx create-snowpack-app todo-ts --template @snowpack/app-\
template-blank-typescript
```

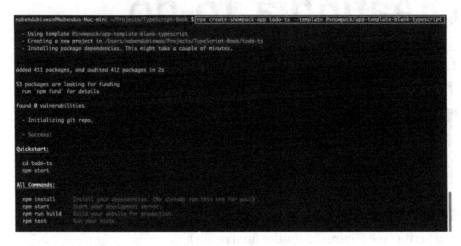

Figure 7-1. *Creating a snowpack project*

That command will create the basic structure. Then, you need to run
the npm start command to start the project on http://localhost:8080/
in the browser. See Figure 7-2.

Figure 7-2. *The starting project*

Next, you need to do some cleanup by deleting all the content from index.ts file. Also delete the files shown in Figure 7-3 from the public folder.

Figure 7-3. *Deleting unnecessary files*

Creating the To-Do List

Remove everything from the index.html file and add the contents of Listing 7-1 to it. Note that the <ul> and <form> elements are inside the <body> tag. This example also uses inline styling in the <body> and <ul> tags.

The <form> tag has an input and a button. Notice that the <script> tag is the module type; that's because you will use ES6 imports in this file.

Listing 7-1. Adding the HTML

```
<!DOCTYPE html>
<html lang="en">
  <head>
    <meta charset="utf-8" />
    <link rel="icon" href="/favicon.ico" />
    <meta name="viewport" content="width=device-width,
    initial-scale=1" />
```

```
    <title>Todo TypeScript</title>
  </head>
  <body style="display: grid; place-items: center">
    <ul id="list" style="list-style: none; padding: 0;"></ul>
    <form id="task-form">
      <input type="text" id="task-title">
      <button type="submit">Add</button>
    </form>
    <script src="dist/index.js" type="module"></script>
  </body>
</html>
```

Now, install the uuid and @types/uuid packages in the project, as shown in Figure 7-4.

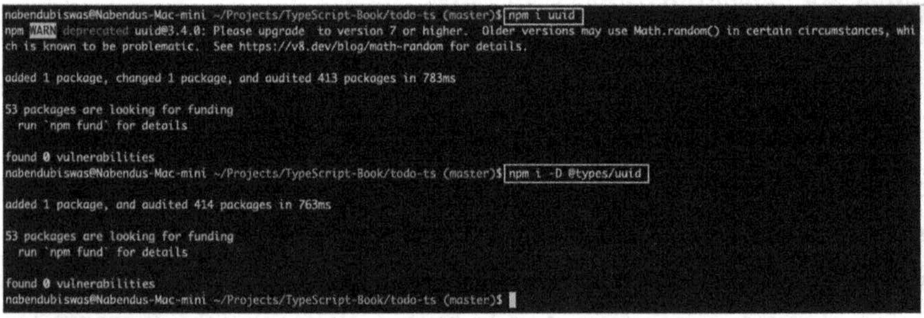

Figure 7-4. *Installing npm packages*

In the index.ts file, import the uuid first, which generates random numbers. After that, you select the <ul>, <form>, and <input> tags. Notice the types that are used for the input elements, which you learned about in an earlier section.

After that, you have an event listener on the form. Notice that optionals are used here, which is another TypeScript feature discussed in Chapter 2. After that, the code checks if the input value is an empty string or null and returns the result.

The newTask object has an interface that defines its types. Inside this object, the id is defined as uuid, the title is the value entered by the user, completed is initially false, and createdAt is the current date.

Listing 7-2. Creating the index.ts File

```
import { v4 as uuidV4 } from "uuid"

const list = document.querySelector<HTMLUListElement>("#list")
const form = document.querySelector<HTMLFormElement>(
"#task-form")
const input = document.querySelector<HTMLInputElement>(
"#task-title")

interface Task {
    id: string
    title: string
    completed: boolean
    createdAt: Date
}

form?.addEventListener("submit", e => {
    e.preventDefault()
    if (input?.value == "" || input?.value == null) return

    const newTask: Task = {
        id: uuidV4(),
        title: input.value,
        completed: false,
        createdAt: new Date()
    }
})
```

Now, create a new function called addItemToList. It will take this task and create a list item, label, and checkbox. Now, if you enter an item and click Add, it will be shown. See Listing 7-3.

Listing 7-3. Adding a Function

```
form?.addEventListener("submit", e => {
    e.preventDefault()
    if (input?.value == "" || input?.value == null) return

    const newTask: Task = {
        id: uuidV4(),
        title: input.value,
        completed: false,
        createdAt: new Date()
    }

    addItemToList(newTask)
})

const addItemToList = (task: Task): void => {
    const item = document.createElement("li")
    const label = document.createElement("label")
    const checkbox = document.createElement("input")
    checkbox.type = "checkbox"
    label.append(checkbox, task.title)
    item.append(label)
    list?.append(item)
}
```

Upon checking the DOM, you can see the exact structure of this item (see Figure 7-5).

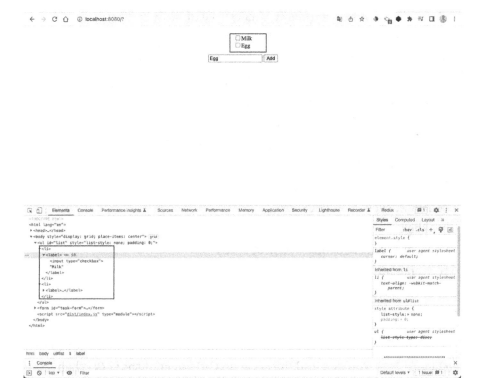

Figure 7-5. *Adding items*

Now, add an event listener inside the `addItemToList` function. In Listing 7-4, you are selecting the checkbox and adding a `line-through` element if the checkbox is selected.

Listing 7-4. Adding Events

```
form?.addEventListener("submit", e => {
    e.preventDefault()
    ...
    addItemToList(newTask)
    input.value = ""
})
```

```
const addItemToList = (task: Task): void => {
  const item = document.createElement("li")
  const label = document.createElement("label")
  const checkbox = document.createElement("input")
  checkbox.addEventListener("change", () => {
    task.completed = checkbox.checked
    if(checkbox.checked) label.style.textDecoration =
    "line-through"
  })
  checkbox.type = "checkbox"
  checkbox.checked = task.completed
  label.append(checkbox, task.title)
  item.append(label)
  list?.append(item)
}
```

This small app is now complete and working perfectly in the localhost (see Figure 7-6). You can find the code on GitHub at `https://github.com/nabendu82/todo-typescript`.

Figure 7-6. *Marking an item*

Summary

In this chapter, you created a simple to-do list app with snowpack. In the next chapter, you will create a fairly big drag-and-drop project.

CHAPTER 8

Creating a Drag-and-Drop Project with TypeScript

In this chapter, you create an awesome drag-and-drop project in TypeScript. It is a fairly large project in comparison to the earlier projects you've tackled so far (see Figure 8-11 for the completed project).

Initial Setup

First, create a new directory called drag-drop and move into it. Inside the drag-drop folder, create a package.json file using the npm init -y command. Also add a tsconfig.json file in this folder using the tsc-init command. See Figure 8-1.

© Nabendu Biswas 2023
N. Biswas, *TypeScript Basics*, https://doi.org/10.1007/978-1-4842-9523-6_8

Figure 8-1. *The directory*

Now, create dist and src folders in the root directory. Inside the src folder, create an index.ts file. Add the code in Listing 8-1 to the index. html file in the root directory.

Listing 8-1. The HTML

```
<!DOCTYPE html>
<html lang="en">
<head>
    <meta charset="UTF-8">
    <meta name="viewport" content="width=device-width,
    initial-scale=1.0">
    <title>Drag and Drop</title>
</head>
<body>
    <script src="dist/index.js"></script>
</body>
</html>
```

In the `tsconfig.json` file, uncomment `rootDir` and `outDir` and provide the appropriate path. See Figure 8-2.

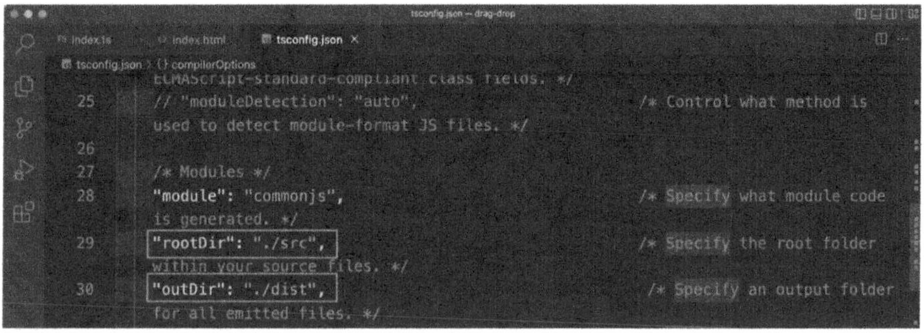

Figure 8-2. *The tsconfig.json updates*

DOM Selection

You will link a `style.css` file to the project by creating it in the root directory. The contents of the file can be taken from the GitHub link listed at the end of the chapter.

In the `index.html` file, you will add a template, and inside that template, you'll add a form. The form will contain `title`, `description`, and `people` input fields and a button. Notice that the form will not be shown in the localhost, because of the template. See Listing 8-2.

Listing 8-2. Adding the First Template

```
<!DOCTYPE html>
<html lang="en">
<head>
    <meta charset="UTF-8">
    <meta name="viewport" content="width=device-width,
    initial-scale=1.0">
```

```html
    <title>Drag and Drop</title>
    <link rel="stylesheet" href="style.css">
</head>
<body>
    <template id="project">
        <form>
            <div class="form-control">
                <label for="title">Title</label>
                <input type="text" id="title" />
            </div>
            <div class="form-control">
                <label for="description">Description</label>
                <textarea id="description" rows="3"></textarea>
            </div>
            <div class="form-control">
                <label for="people">People</label>
                <input type="number" id="people" step="1"
                min="0" max="10" />
            </div>
            <button type="submit">ADD PROJECT</button>
        </form>
    </template>
    <script src="dist/index.js"></script>
</body>
</html>
```

Next, you add two more templates to the project. You also need to start a live server in the project. See Listing 8-3.

Listing 8-3. Adding Another Template

```
      . . .
    . . .
            </form>
      </template>
      <template id="single">
          <li></li>
      </template>
      <template id="list">
          <section class="projects">
              <header>
                  <h2></h2>
              </header>
              <ul></ul>
          </section>
      </template>
      <div id="app"></div>
      <script src="dist/index.js"></script>
</body>
</html>
```

Next, create a `Project` class in the `index.ts` file. Inside the constructor, you first select the template with the project ID. After that, you select the `div` with the `app` ID.

Next, you import the template using `importNode()`. Since the form element is the first element of the template, you store it in `formElem`, with `firstElementChild`.

Next, you attach the method that shows the form in the `div` with the `app` ID.

Notice that this example also starts the TypeScript part with `tsc -w` command. See Listing 8-4.

Listing 8-4. The index.ts File

```
class Project {
    templateElem: HTMLTemplateElement;
    renderElem: HTMLDivElement;
    formElem: HTMLFormElement;

    constructor() {
        this.templateElem = <HTMLTemplateElement>document.
        querySelector('#project');
        this.renderElem = <HTMLDivElement>document.
        querySelector('#app');

        const imported = document.importNode(this.templateElem.
        content, true);
        this.formElem = <HTMLFormElement>imported.
        firstElementChild;
        this.attach();
    }

    private attach(){
        this.renderElem.insertAdjacentElement('afterbegin',
        this.formElem);
    }
}

const project = new Project();
```

Now, you will see a nice-looking form in the localhost, as shown in Figure 8-3.

Figure 8-3. *The output*

Now you need to add some elements for selection. You also call the config() function from the constructor. In the config() function, you add an event listener to the form and show the title entered by the user. See Listing 8-5.

Listing 8-5. Adding More Elements

```
class Project {
    templateElem: HTMLTemplateElement;
    renderElem: HTMLDivElement;
    formElem: HTMLFormElement;
    titleElem: HTMLInputElement;
    descElem: HTMLInputElement;
    peopleElem: HTMLInputElement;

    constructor() {
        this.templateElem = <HTMLTemplateElement>document.
        querySelector('#project');
        this.renderElem = <HTMLDivElement>document.
        querySelector('#app');
```

```
        const imported = document.importNode(this.templateElem.
        content, true);
        this.formElem = <HTMLFormElement>imported.
        firstElementChild;
        this.formElem.id = 'user-input';
        this.titleElem = <HTMLInputElement>this.formElem.
        querySelector('#title');
        this.descElem = <HTMLInputElement>this.formElem.
        querySelector('#description');
        this.peopleElem = <HTMLInputElement>this.formElem.
        querySelector('#people');
        this.config();
        this.attach();
    }

    private config() {
        this.formElem.addEventListener('submit', e => {
            e.preventDefault();
            console.log(this.titleElem.value);
        })
    }
    ...
      ...
}
```

Now, enter something in the title and click the Add Project button. Figure 8-4 shows some entered text in the console log.

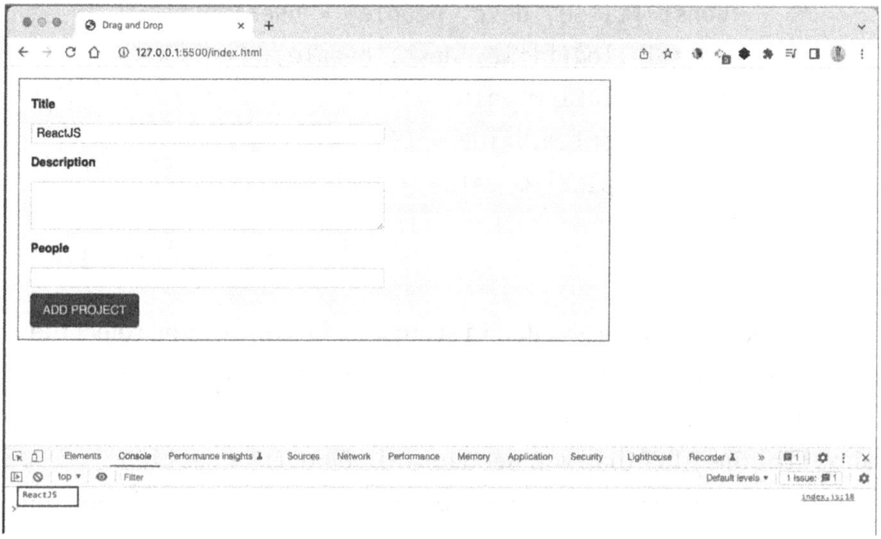

Figure 8-4. *The console log*

Rendering a List

In this section, you will create a `userInput` array and add `title`, `description`, and `people` to it. You also create the `title`, `desc`, and `people` variables and assign them by array-destructuring of `userInput`.

After that, you need to make the elements an empty string so that the user-entered data is cleared after clicking Submit. See Listing 8-6.

Listing 8-6. Adding More Data

```
private config() {
    this.formElem.addEventListener('submit', e => {
        e.preventDefault();
        let userInput:[string, string, number] = [this.
        titleElem.value, this.descElem.value, +this.
        peopleElem.value];
```

```
        const [title, desc, people] = userInput;
        console.log(title, desc, people);
        this.titleElem.value = '';
        this.descElem.value = '';
        this.peopleElem.value = '';
    })
  }
```

Now create a new class called List. Inside the constructor, select the template with the list ID. Then select the section inside it.

Next, select the section element, which is inside this template in the index.html file. After that, you need to add a type ID for section.

Then attach it to the div with the app ID, using the attach() function. After that in, the listId and the two types of projects will then appear in contentRender().

You changed the earlier class called Project to Input. You also created an instance of Input and two instances of List, with active and finished being passed for constructors. See Listing 8-7.

Listing 8-7. Adding a List

```
class List {
    templateElem: HTMLTemplateElement;
    renderElem: HTMLDivElement;
    sectionElem: HTMLElement;

    constructor(private type: 'active' | 'finished') {
        this.templateElem = <HTMLTemplateElement>document.
        querySelector('#list');
        this.renderElem = <HTMLDivElement>document.
        querySelector('#app');
        const imported = document.importNode(this.templateElem.
        content, true);
```

```
        this.sectionElem = <HTMLElement>imported.
        firstElementChild;
        this.sectionElem.id = '${this.type}-projects';
        this.attach();
        this.contentRender();
    }

    private contentRender() {
        const listId = '${this.type}-projects-list';
        this.sectionElem.querySelector('ul')!.id = listId;
        this.sectionElem.querySelector('h2')!.innerText =
        '${this.type.toUpperCase()} PROJECTS';
    }

    private attach(){
        this.renderElem.insertAdjacentElement('beforeend',
        this.sectionElem);
    }
}

class Input {
 ...
 ...
}

const projInput = new Input();
const activeList = new List('active');
const finishedList = new List('finished');
```

Now you can see the Active and Finished projects in the localhost, as shown in Figure 8-5.

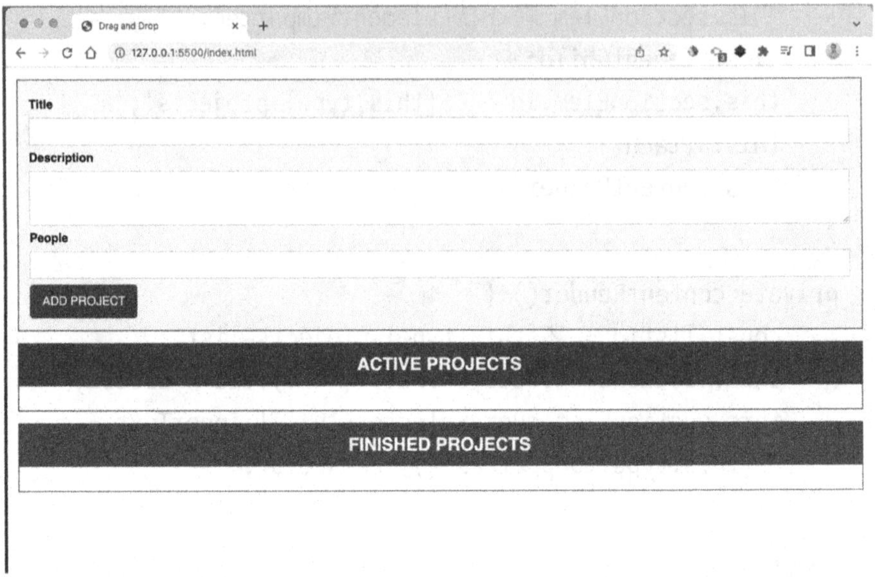

Figure 8-5. *The current project*

You now need to create a class called State. It is a Singleton class with a private constructor. It has two functions—addListener and addProject. The addListener function adds listenerFn to the listeners array.

To the addProject function, you need to add a new project in the projects array. See Listing 8-8.

Listing 8-8. The Singleton Class

```
class State {
    private listeners: any[] = [];
    private projects: any[] = [];
    private static instance: State;
    private constructor() {}
    static getInstance() {
        if (this.instance) return this.instance;
```

```
        this.instance = new State();
        return this.instance;
    }

    addListener(listenerFn: Function){
        this.listeners.push(listenerFn);
    }

    addProject(title: string, desc: string, nums: number) {
        const newProject = {
            id: Math.random().toString(),
            title: title,
            description: desc,
            people: nums
        };
        this.projects.push(newProject);
        for (const listenerFn of this.listeners) {
            listenerFn(this.projects.slice());
        }
    }
}

const prjState = State.getInstance();
```

Back in the List class, create an assignedProjects array. After that, add a listener for each project by using the addListener function of the State class.

Next, you render each of the projects by looping through the assignedProjects array. Create an <li> inside the <ul> you created earlier. See Listing 8-9.

Listing 8-9. Updating the List

```
class List {
    templateElem: HTMLTemplateElement;
    renderElem: HTMLDivElement;
    sectionElem: HTMLElement;
    assignedProjects: any[];

    constructor(private type: 'active' | 'finished') {
        this.templateElem = <HTMLTemplateElement>document.
        querySelector('#list');
        this.renderElem = <HTMLDivElement>document.
        querySelector('#app');
        this.assignedProjects = [];
        const imported = document.importNode(this.templateElem.
        content, true);
        this.sectionElem = <HTMLElement>imported.
        firstElementChild;
        this.sectionElem.id = '${this.type}-projects';
        prjState.addListener((projects: any[]) => {
            this.assignedProjects = projects;
            this.projectsRender();
        })
        this.attach();
        this.contentRender();
    }

    private projectsRender() {
        const listEl = <HTMLUListElement>document.
        getElementById('${this.type}-projects-list');
        for (const prjItem of this.assignedProjects) {
            const listItem = document.createElement('li');
            listItem.textContent = prjItem.title;
```

```
        listEl.appendChild(listItem);
      }
    }
}
```

In `config()` function that's inside the `Input` class, you call the `addProject` function with `title`, `desc`, and `people`. See Listing 8-10.

Listing 8-10. Updating the Input

```
class Input {
    ...
    ...
    private config() {
        this.formElem.addEventListener('submit', e => {
            e.preventDefault();
            let userInput:[string, string, number] = [this.
            titleElem.value, this.descElem.value, +this.
            peopleElem.value];
            const [title, desc, people] = userInput;
            prjState.addProject(title, desc, people);
            this.titleElem.value = '';
            this.descElem.value = '';
            this.peopleElem.value = '';
        })
    }
}
```

If you now add a new title and click Add Project, you will see the title in the Active and Finished projects. You have to fix some bugs and add filtering logic next (see Figure 8-6).

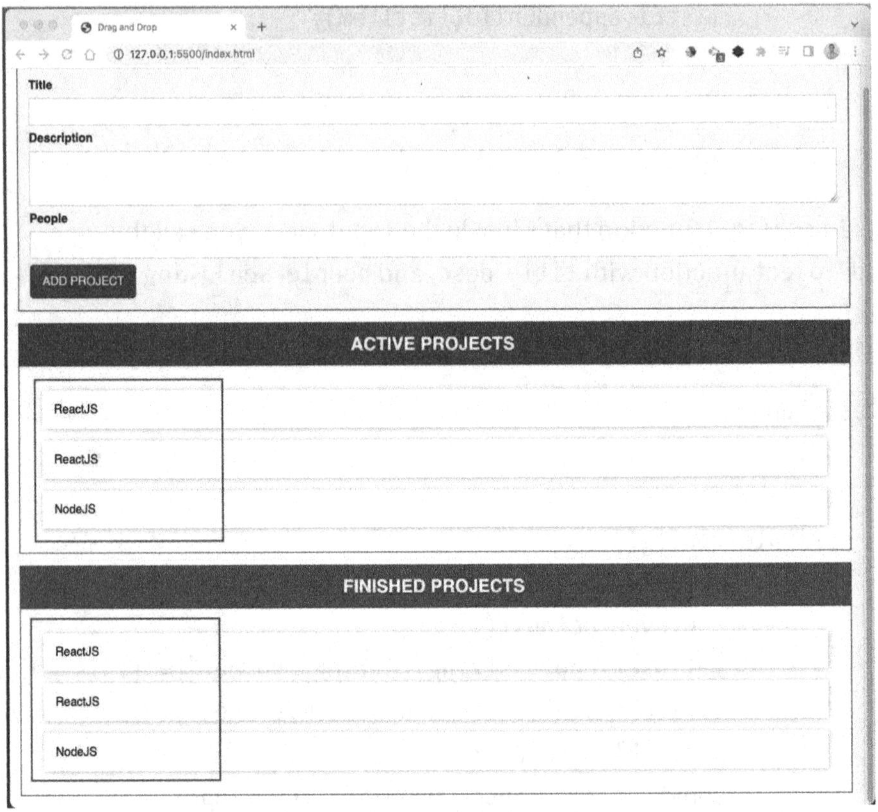

Figure 8-6. *The bug*

Filtering Logic

In this section, you create a new class called Project. Add the id, title, description, people, and status features to the constructor. The status is an enum called ProjectStatus with an Active or Finished state.

You also need to change the earlier type called any to Project and create an instance of Project and pass the required parameters to it. See Listing 8-11.

Listing 8-11. Adding the Project Class

```typescript
enum ProjectStatus {
    Active,
    Finished
}

class Project {
    constructor(public id: string, public title: string, public
    description: string, public people: number,public status:
    ProjectStatus) { }
}

class State {
    private listeners: any[] = [];
    private projects: Project[] = [];
    private static instance: State;
    private constructor() {}
      ..
    addProject(title: string, desc: string, nums: number) {
        const newProject = new Project( Math.random().
        toString(), title, desc, nums, ProjectStatus.Active);
        this.projects.push(newProject);
        for (const listenerFn of this.listeners) {
            listenerFn(this.projects.slice());
        }
    }
}
```

In the List class, replace the earlier type called any with the Project type. See Listing 8-12.

Listing 8-12. Updating the List

```
class List {
    templateElem: HTMLTemplateElement;
    renderElem: HTMLDivElement;
    sectionElem: HTMLElement;
    assignedProjects: Project[];

    constructor(private type: 'active' | 'finished') {
        ...
        prjState.addListener((projects: Project[]) => {
            this.assignedProjects = projects;
            this.projectsRender();
        })
        this.attach();
        this.contentRender();
    }
    ...
    ...
}
```

Next, you need to create a type called Listener and make the earlier type called any the Listener type in the State class. See Listing 8-13.

Listing 8-13. Updating the State Class

```
type Listener = (items: Project[]) => void;

class State {
    private listeners: Listener[] = [];
    private projects: Project[] = [];
    ...
    ...
```

```typescript
    addListener(listenerFn: Listener){
        this.listeners.push(listenerFn);
    }
    ...
}
```

Add the filtering logic to the List class. As Listing 8-14 shows, you add the Active or Finished status based on the status.

Listing 8-14. Updating the List Class

```typescript
class List {
    ...

    constructor(private type: 'active' | 'finished') {
        ...
        this.sectionElem.id = '${this.type}-projects';
        prjState.addListener((projects: Project[]) => {
            const relevantProjects = projects.filter(prj
            => this.type === 'active' ? prj.status
            === ProjectStatus.Active : prj.status ===
            ProjectStatus.Finished);
            this.assignedProjects = relevantProjects;
            this.projectsRender();
        })
        this.attach();
        this.contentRender();
    }

    private projectsRender() {
        const listEl = <HTMLUListElement>document.
        getElementById('${this.type}-projects-list');
        listEl.innerHTML = '';
```

```
      for (const prjItem of this.assignedProjects) {
          const listItem = document.createElement('li');
          listItem.textContent = prjItem.title;
          listEl.appendChild(listItem);
      }
    }
    ...
}
}
```

Now, all the new projects will go to the Active Projects list, as shown in Figure 8-7.

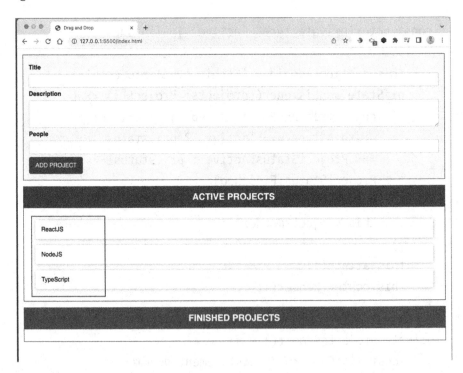

Figure 8-7. *Titles have been added*

Abstract Class

These are common functionalities in the List and Item classes, which you will move to an abstract class called Component.

Listing 8-15 moves the common functionalities of template, render, and element. The attach method is now taking an insert parameter, because you have two types of it in the List and Item classes.

Two abstract methods—called configure() and contentRender()— need to be created by the classes that will inherit from the Component class.

Listing 8-15. An Abstract Class

```
// Component Base Class
abstract class Component<T extends HTMLElement, U extends
HTMLElement> {
    templateElem: HTMLTemplateElement;
    renderElem: T;
    element: U;

    constructor(templateId: string, renderElemId: string,
    insertAtStart: boolean, newElemId?: string) {
        this.templateElem = document.
        getElementById(templateId)! as HTMLTemplateElement;
        this.renderElem = document.
        getElementById(renderElemId)! as T;
        const importedNode = document.importNode(this.
        templateElem.content, true);
        this.element = importedNode.firstElementChild as U;
        if (newElemId) this.element.id = newElemId;
        this.attach(insertAtStart);
    }
```

```
    private attach(insert: boolean) {
        this.renderElem.insertAdjacentElement(insert ?
        'afterbegin' : 'beforeend', this.element);
    }

    abstract configure(): void;
    abstract contentRender(): void;
}
```

Now, in the List class, you extend the Component. Listing 8-16 has removed all the earlier code from the constructor and passed it to the Component class using super(). It also passes the earlier filter logic to configure().

Listing 8-16. List Class Has Been Updated

```
class List extends Component<HTMLDivElement, HTMLElement> {
    assignedProjects: Project[];

    constructor(private type: 'active' | 'finished'){
        super('list', 'app', false, '${type}-projects');
        this.assignedProjects = [];
        this.configure();
        this.contentRender();
    }

    configure(){
        prjState.addListener((projects: Project[]) => {
            const relevantProjects = projects.filter(prj =>
            this.type === 'active' ? prj.status ===
            ProjectStatus.Active : prj.status ===
            ProjectStatus.Finished);
            this.assignedProjects = relevantProjects;
```

```
            this.projectsRender();
        })
    }

    contentRender() {
        const listId = '${this.type}-projects-list';
        this.element.querySelector('ul')!.id = listId;
        this.element.querySelector('h2')!.innerText = '${this.
        type.toUpperCase()} PROJECTS';
    }

    private projectsRender() {
        const listEl = <HTMLUListElement>document.
        getElementById('${this.type}-projects-list');
        listEl.innerHTML = '';
        for (const prjItem of this.assignedProjects) {
            const listItem = document.createElement('li');
            listItem.textContent = prjItem.title;
            listEl.appendChild(listItem);
        }
    }
}
```

Listing 8-17 extends the Component, this time in the Input class. The earlier code has been removed from the constructor and is passed to the Component class using super(). The earlier submit logic has also been passed to configure().

Listing 8-17. Input Class Has Been Updated

```
class Input extends Component<HTMLDivElement,
HTMLFormElement> {
    titleElem: HTMLInputElement;
    descElem: HTMLInputElement;
```

```
    peopleElem: HTMLInputElement;

    constructor() {
        super('project', 'app', true, 'user-input');
        this.titleElem = <HTMLInputElement>this.element.
        querySelector('#title');
        this.descElem = <HTMLInputElement>this.element.
        querySelector('#description');
        this.peopleElem = <HTMLInputElement>this.element.
        querySelector('#people');
        this.configure();
    }

    configure() {
        this.element.addEventListener('submit', e => {
            e.preventDefault();
            let userInput:[string, string, number] = [this.
            titleElem.value, this.descElem.value, +this.
            peopleElem.value];
            const [title, desc, people] = userInput;
            prjState.addProject(title, desc, people);
            this.titleElem.value = '';
            this.descElem.value = '';
            this.peopleElem.value = '';
        })
    }

    contentRender() {}
}
```

Listing 8-18 performs further optimization by putting addListener in its own ListenerState class.

Listing 8-18. ListenerState Class

```typescript
type Listener<T> = (items: T[]) => void;

class ListenerState<T> {
    protected listeners: Listener<T>[] = [];

    addListener(listenerFn: Listener<T>) {
        this.listeners.push(listenerFn);
    }
}

class State extends ListenerState<Project> {
    private projects: Project[] = [];
    private static instance: State;
    private constructor() {
            super()
    }
    static getInstance() {
        if (this.instance) return this.instance;
        this.instance = new State();
        return this.instance;
    }

    addProject(title: string, desc: string, nums: number) {
    ...
    ...
    }
}
```

Upon checking in the localhost (see Figure 8-8), you can see that the titles were added properly.

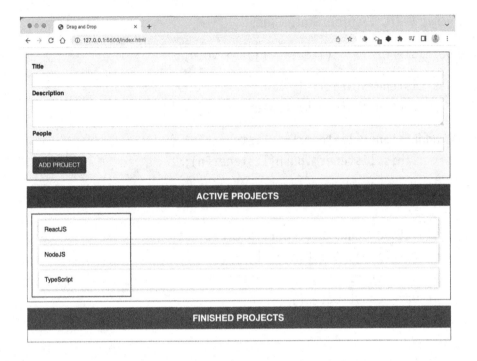

Figure 8-8. *Everything is working*

Rendering Items

Listing 8-19 creates <h2>, <h3>, and <p> tags inside the <li> tag of the single template.

Listing 8-19. Template Update

```
<template id="single">
        <li>
        <h2></h2>
        <h3></h3>
        <p></p>
        </li>
</template>
```

Now, you can create a new Item class, which will again extend from Component. You again pass the required code from super(). In contentRender(), you assign the <h2>, <h3>, and <pr> tags with the respective fields.

Listing 8-20 also creates a getter, called persons. It will return 1 person or a number of persons, depending on the people assigned to the project.

Listing 8-20. The Item Class

```
class Item extends Component<HTMLUListElement, HTMLLIElement> {
    private project: Project;

    get persons() {
        return this.project.people === 1 ? '1 person' :
        '${this.project.people} persons';
    }

    constructor(hostId: string, project: Project) {
        super('single', hostId, false, project.id);
        this.project = project;

        this.configure();
        this.contentRender();
    }

    configure(){}

    contentRender(){
        this.element.querySelector('h2')!.innerText = this.
        project.title;
        this.element.querySelector('h3')!.innerText = this.
        persons + ' assigned';
        this.element.querySelector('p')!.innerText = this.
        project.description;
    }
}
```

Now, from the List class, you need to instantiate the Item class with id and prjItem. See Listing 8-21.

Listing 8-21. List Class Has Been Updated

```
class List extends Component<HTMLDivElement, HTMLElement> {
    . . .
    . . .
    private projectsRender() {
        const listEl = <HTMLUListElement>document.
        getElementById('${this.type}-projects-list');
        listEl.innerHTML = '';
        for (const prjItem of this.assignedProjects) {
            new Item(this.element.querySelector('ul')!.id,
            prjItem);
        }
    }
}
```

Upon adding a project with the required fields, you will see that all the fields are working, as shown in Figure 8-9.

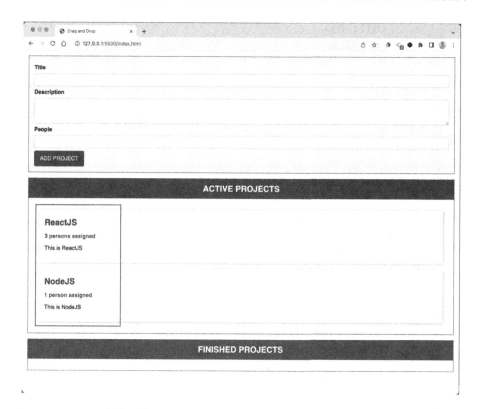

Figure 8-9. *All fields are working*

Draggable Items

In this section, you learn how to create the main logic of the draggable items from Active Projects to Finished Projects. First, you need to add the HTML property called `draggable` to the list item, as shown in Listing 8-22.

Listing 8-22. Draggable Has Been Added

```
<template id="single">
    <li draggable="true">
        <h2></h2>
```

```
            <h3></h3>
            <p></p>
        </li>
    </template>
```

Next, you create the interface for Draggable and DragTarget in the index.ts file, as shown in Listing 8-23.

Listing 8-23. Interface Has Been Added

```
interface Draggable {
    dragStartHandler(event: DragEvent): void;
    dragEndHandler(event: DragEvent): void;
}

interface DragTarget {
    dragOverHandler(event: DragEvent): void;
    dropHandler(event: DragEvent): void;
    dragLeaveHandler(event: DragEvent): void;
}
```

You need to implement Draggable in the Item class. After that, you add the dragStartHandler and dragEndHandler methods to it.

In the configure() method, you need to add the dragstart and dragend event listeners to each element. These event listeners will call the dragStartHandler and dragEndHandler methods, respectively. See Listing 8-24.

Listing 8-24. Draggable Has Been Implemented

```
class Item extends Component<HTMLUListElement, HTMLLIElement>
implements Draggable {
    private project: Project;
```

```typescript
get persons() {
    return this.project.people === 1 ? '1 person' :
    '${this.project.people} persons';
}

constructor(hostId: string, project: Project) {
    super('single', hostId, false, project.id);
    this.project = project;

    this.configure();
    this.contentRender();
}

dragStartHandler = (event: DragEvent) => {
    console.log('DragStart', event);
}

dragEndHandler = (_: DragEvent) => {
    console.log('DragEnd');
}

configure(){
    this.element.addEventListener('dragstart', this.
    dragStartHandler);
    this.element.addEventListener('dragend', this.
    dragEndHandler);
}
...
}
```

Now, when you drag an item to Active Projects, this action will be shown in the console, as you can see in Figure 8-10.

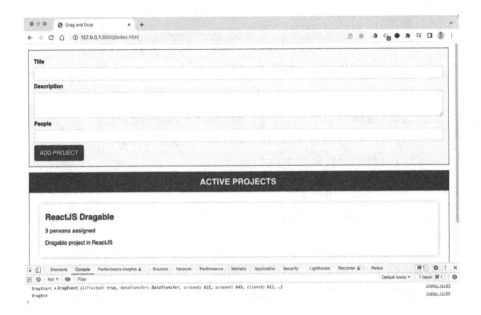

Figure 8-10. *Draggable*

Next, in the `dragStartHandler` method, you call the `setData` function from the event and pass `id` to it. You also need to set `effectAllowed` to true. See Listing 8-25.

Listing 8-25. dragStartHandler Has Been Updated

```
dragStartHandler = (event: DragEvent) => {
    event.dataTransfer!.setData('text/plain', this.
    project.id);
    event.dataTransfer!.effectAllowed = 'move';
}
```

Create a new function called `moveProject` in the `State` class. From the list of all the projects, you can find the project being dragged with the project ID.

Inside that project, change the project status and call a new function called updateListeners, which will re-create all the listeners. See Listing 8-26.

Listing 8-26. State Has Been Updated

```
class State extends ListenerState<Project> {
    ...
    addProject(title: string, desc: string, nums: number) {
        const newProject = new Project( Math.random().
        toString(), title, desc, nums, ProjectStatus.Active);
        this.projects.push(newProject);
        this.updateListeners();
    }

    moveProject(projectId: string, newStatus: ProjectStatus) {
        const project = this.projects.find(prj => prj.id ===
        projectId);
        if (project && project.status !== newStatus) {
            project.status = newStatus;
            this.updateListeners();
        }
    }

    private updateListeners() {
        for (const listenerFn of this.listeners) {
            listenerFn(this.projects.slice());
        }
    }
}
```

Now you need to implement Dragtarget in the List class. Call the dragOverHandler, dragLeaveHandler, and dropHandler functions from the dragover, dragleave, and drop events, respectively.

In the dragOverHandler function, add the class called droppable to the
<ul> containing the item.

In the dragLeaveHandler function, remove the class called droppable.

In the dropHandler function, call moveProject and pass the item ID
and the status. See Listing 8-27.

Listing 8-27. List Has Been Updated

```
class List extends Component<HTMLDivElement, HTMLElement>
implements DragTarget {
    ...
    dragOverHandler = (event: DragEvent) => {
        if (event.dataTransfer && event.dataTransfer.types[0]
        === 'text/plain') {
            event.preventDefault();
            const listEl = this.element.querySelector('ul')!;
            listEl.classList.add('droppable');
        }
    }

    dropHandler = (event: DragEvent) => {
        const prjId = event.dataTransfer!.getData('text/
        plain');
        prjState.moveProject(
            prjId,
            this.type === 'active' ? ProjectStatus.Active :
            ProjectStatus.Finished
        );
    }

    dragLeaveHandler = (_: DragEvent) => {
        const listEl = this.element.querySelector('ul')!;
        listEl.classList.remove('droppable');
    }
```

```
configure(){
    this.element.addEventListener('dragover', this.
    dragOverHandler);
    this.element.addEventListener('dragleave', this.
    dragLeaveHandler);
    this.element.addEventListener('drop', this.
    dropHandler);
    prjState.addListener((projects: Project[]) => {
        const relevantProjects = projects.filter(prj =>
        this.type === 'active' ? prj.status ===
        ProjectStatus.Active : prj.status ===
        ProjectStatus.Finished);
        this.assignedProjects = relevantProjects;
        this.projectsRender();
    })
}
...
}
```

The final project is done, and you can now drag items from Active to Finished projects (see Figure 8-11).

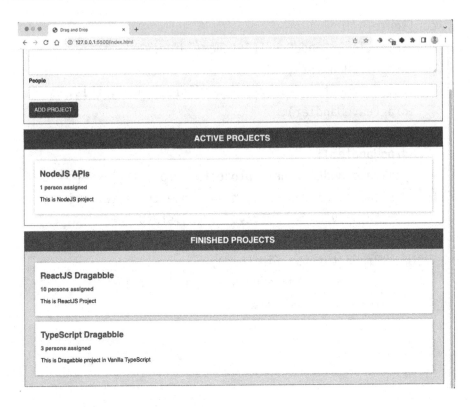

Figure 8-11. *The final project*

You can find the code for this project on GitHub at `https://github.com/nabendu82/drag-drop-ts`.

Summary

In this chapter, you created a fairly complex TypeScript app for tracking projects. The final app has draggable projects, which can be dragged from the Active to Finished status. In the next chapter, you learn how to divide this large project into small, manageable modules.

CHAPTER 9

Improving the Drag-and-Drop Project

The drag-and-drop project you created in the previous chapter is a large `index.ts` file. In this chapter, you are first going to divide the project into small, manageable modules (see Figure 9-1). After that, you are also going to learn about webpack and make the project more efficient (Figure 9-8 shows the end result).

Changing to ES6 Modules

The first thing you need to do is add a module to the script file in `index.html`, as shown in Listing 9-1.

Listing 9-1. Adding a Module

```
<script type="module" src="dist/index.js"></script>
```

Now, create a `models` folder inside the `src` folder and create two files—`drag.ts` and `project.ts`—inside that folder.

Place the interface code from `index.ts` into the `drag.ts` file, as shown in Listing 9-2. The only difference is the `export` at the front.

© Nabendu Biswas 2023
N. Biswas, *TypeScript Basics*, https://doi.org/10.1007/978-1-4842-9523-6_9

Listing 9-2. Creating the drag.ts File

```
export interface Draggable {
    dragStartHandler(event: DragEvent): void;
    dragEndHandler(event: DragEvent): void;
}

export interface DragTarget {
    dragOverHandler(event: DragEvent): void;
    dropHandler(event: DragEvent): void;
    dragLeaveHandler(event: DragEvent): void;
}
```

Next, in the project.ts file, export the Project class and the ProjectStatus enum, again from the index.ts file. See Listing 9-3.

Listing 9-3. Creating the project.ts File

```
export enum ProjectStatus {
    Active,
    Finished
}

export class Project {
    constructor(public id: string, public title: string, public
    description: string, public people: number,public status:
    ProjectStatus) { }
}
```

Create a state folder inside the src folder and add a state.ts file in that new folder. Inside it, transfer State and ListenerState from index. ts. Note that this example also imports Project and ProjectStatus from the project.ts file. See Listing 9-4.

Listing 9-4. Creating the state.ts File

```
import { Project, ProjectStatus } from '../models/project.js';

type Listener<T> = (items: T[]) => void;
class ListenerState<T> {
    protected listeners: Listener<T>[] = [];
    addListener(listenerFn: Listener<T>) {
        this.listeners.push(listenerFn);
    }
}

class State extends ListenerState<Project> {
    private projects: Project[] = [];
    private static instance: State;
    private constructor() {
        super()
    }
    static getInstance() {
        if (this.instance) return this.instance;
        this.instance = new State();
        return this.instance;
    }

    addProject(title: string, desc: string, nums: number) {
        const newProject = new Project( Math.random().
        toString(), title, desc, nums, ProjectStatus.Active);
        this.projects.push(newProject);
        this.updateListeners();
    }

    moveProject(projectId: string, newStatus: ProjectStatus) {
        const project = this.projects.find(prj => prj.id ===
        projectId);
```

```
        if (project && project.status !== newStatus) {
            project.status = newStatus;
            this.updateListeners();
        }
    }

    private updateListeners() {
        for (const listenerFn of this.listeners) {
            listenerFn(this.projects.slice());
        }
    }
}

export const prjState = State.getInstance();
```

Now, create a components folder inside the src folder and a base.ts file to that new folder. In Listing 9-5, you are transferring the Component abstract class from the index.ts file.

Listing 9-5. Creating the base.ts File

```
export default abstract class Component<T extends HTMLElement,
U extends HTMLElement> {
    templateElem: HTMLTemplateElement;
    renderElem: T;
    element: U;

    constructor(templateId: string, renderElemId: string,
    insertAtStart: boolean, newElemId?: string) {
        this.templateElem = document.
        getElementById(templateId)! as HTMLTemplateElement;
        this.renderElem = document.
        getElementById(renderElemId)! as T;
```

```
    const importedNode = document.importNode(this.
    templateElem.content, true);
    this.element = importedNode.firstElementChild as U;
    if (newElemId) this.element.id = newElemId;
    this.attach(insertAtStart);
  }

  private attach(insert: boolean) {
    this.renderElem.insertAdjacentElement(insert ?
    'afterbegin' : 'beforeend', this.element);
  }

  abstract configure(): void;
  abstract contentRender(): void;
}
```

Next, create an item.ts file inside the components folder. Transfer
the Item class from the index.ts file. As you can see in Listing 9-6, the
necessary imports are also included.

Listing 9-6. Creating the item.ts File

```
import { Draggable } from "../models/drag.js";
import { Project } from "../models/project.js";
import Component from "./base.js";

export class Item extends Component<HTMLULIstElement,
HTMLLIElement> implements Draggable {
  private project: Project;

  get persons() {
    return this.project.people === 1 ? '1 person' :
    '${this.project.people} persons';
  }
```

```
constructor(hostId: string, project: Project) {
    super('single', hostId, false, project.id);
    this.project = project;

    this.configure();
    this.contentRender();
}

dragStartHandler = (event: DragEvent) => {
    event.dataTransfer!.setData('text/plain', this.
    project.id);
    event.dataTransfer!.effectAllowed = 'move';
}

dragEndHandler = (_: DragEvent) => {
    console.log('DragEnd');
}

configure(){
    this.element.addEventListener('dragstart', this.
    dragStartHandler);
    this.element.addEventListener('dragend', this.
    dragEndHandler);
}

contentRender(){
    this.element.querySelector('h2')!.innerText = this.
    project.title;
    this.element.querySelector('h3')!.innerText = this.
    persons + ' assigned';
    this.element.querySelector('p')!.innerText = this.
    project.description;
}
}
```

Now, create a list.ts file inside the components folder. Transfer the List class from index.ts. As you can see in Listing 9-7, the necessary imports are also included.

Listing 9-7. Creating the list.ts File

```
import { DragTarget } from "../models/drag.js";
import { Project, ProjectStatus } from "../models/project.js";
import Component from "./base.js";
import { prjState } from "../state/state.js";
import { Item } from "./item.js";

export class List extends Component<HTMLDivElement,
HTMLElement> implements DragTarget {
    assignedProjects: Project[];

    constructor(private type: 'active' | 'finished'){
        super('list', 'app', false, '${type}-projects');
        this.assignedProjects = [];
        this.configure();
        this.contentRender();
    }

    dragOverHandler = (event: DragEvent) => {
        if (event.dataTransfer && event.dataTransfer.types[0]
        === 'text/plain') {
            event.preventDefault();
            const listEl = this.element.querySelector('ul')!;
            listEl.classList.add('droppable');
        }
    }
}
```

```
dropHandler = (event: DragEvent) => {
    const prjId = event.dataTransfer!.getData('text/plain');
    prjState.moveProject(
        prjId,
        this.type === 'active' ? ProjectStatus.Active :
        ProjectStatus.Finished
    );
}

dragLeaveHandler = (_: DragEvent) => {
    const listEl = this.element.querySelector('ul')!;
    listEl.classList.remove('droppable');
}

configure(){
    this.element.addEventListener('dragover', this.
    dragOverHandler);
    this.element.addEventListener('dragleave', this.
    dragLeaveHandler);
    this.element.addEventListener('drop', this.dropHandler);
    prjState.addListener((projects: Project[]) => {
        const relevantProjects = projects.filter(prj
        => this.type === 'active' ? prj.status
        === ProjectStatus.Active : prj.status ===
        ProjectStatus.Finished);
        this.assignedProjects = relevantProjects;
        this.projectsRender();
    })
}

contentRender() {
    const listId = '${this.type}-projects-list';
    this.element.querySelector('ul')!.id = listId;
```

```
    this.element.querySelector('h2')!.innerText = '${this.
    type.toUpperCase()} PROJECTS';
}

private projectsRender() {
    const listEl = <HTMLUListElement>document.
    getElementById('${this.type}-projects-list');
    listEl.innerHTML = '';
    for (const prjItem of this.assignedProjects) {
        new Item(this.element.querySelector('ul')!.id,
        prjItem);
    }
}
}
```

Now, create an input.ts file inside the components folder. Transfer the Input class from index.ts. As you can see in Listing 9-8, the necessary imports are also included.

Listing 9-8. Creating the input.ts File

```
import { prjState } from "../state/state.js";
import Component from "./base.js";

export class Input extends Component<HTMLDivElement,
HTMLFormElement> {
    titleElem: HTMLInputElement;
    descElem: HTMLInputElement;
    peopleElem: HTMLInputElement;

    constructor() {
        super('project', 'app', true, 'user-input');
        this.titleElem = <HTMLInputElement>this.element.
        querySelector('#title');
```

```
        this.descElem = <HTMLInputElement>this.element.
        querySelector('#description');
        this.peopleElem = <HTMLInputElement>this.element.
        querySelector('#people');
        this.configure();
    }

    configure() {
        this.element.addEventListener('submit', e => {
            e.preventDefault();
            let userInput:[string, string, number] = [this.
            titleElem.value, this.descElem.value, +this.
            peopleElem.value];
            const [title, desc, people] = userInput;
            prjState.addProject(title, desc, people);
            this.titleElem.value = '';
            this.descElem.value = '';
            this.peopleElem.value = '';
        })
    }

    contentRender() {}
}
```

Finally in the index.ts file, you only import twice and keep the instantiating of classes, as shown in Listing 9-9.

Listing 9-9. Updating the index.ts File

```
import { Input } from './components/input.js';
import { List } from './components/list.js';

new Input();
new List('active');
new List('finished');
```

You also need to change module to es2015 in the tsconfig.json file, as shown in Listing 9-10. Finally, start the project using the tsc -w command.

Listing 9-10. Updating the tsconfig.json File

```
"module": "es2015",
```

Upon checking the project on the localhost, you will see that it works (see Figure 9-1). You can find this code on GitHub at https://github.com/nabendu82/drag-drop-ts-v2.

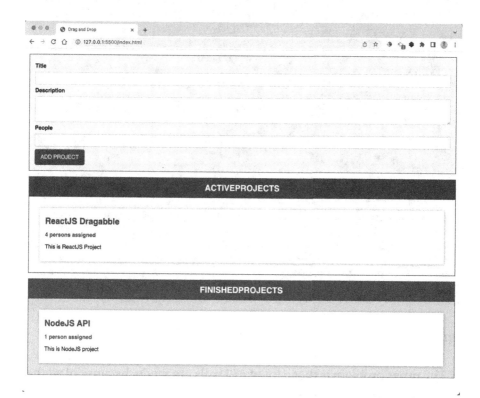

Figure 9-1. *The enhanced project*

Using Webpack

In this optimized project with modules, you have two problems. First, the dist folder is an exact replica of the src folder. It includes all the JavaScript files, corresponding with the TypeScript files. Because of this, the code is not optimized (see Figure 9-2).

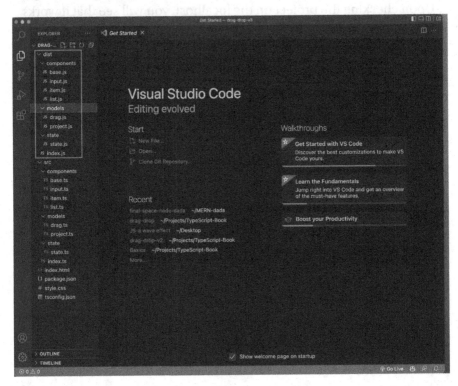

Figure 9-2. *The code is not optimized*

The other problem is that a lot of API calls are made, because of all the different files. You can see this on the Network tab shown in Figure 9-3.

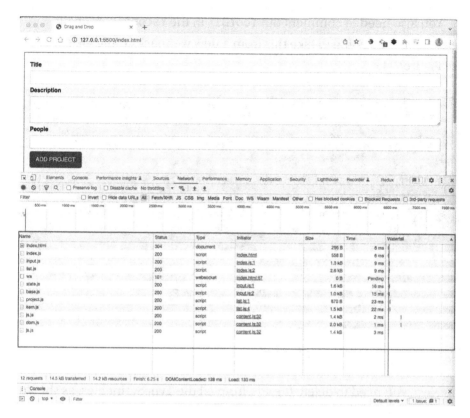

Figure 9-3. *The Network tab*

To solve these issues, it's best to use a bundler like webpack. It changes the TypeScript files into a single, optimized JavaScript file. The production app will then be optimized and thus be faster.

To use webpack in your project, you need to add webpack along with its dependencies, as shown in Listing 9-11.

Listing 9-11. Installing webpack

```
npm i -D webpack webpack-cli webpack-dev-server typescript
ts-loader
```

You also need to comment out rootDir in the tsconfig.json file, because you are going to take this from a new webpack config file soon. See Figure 9-4.

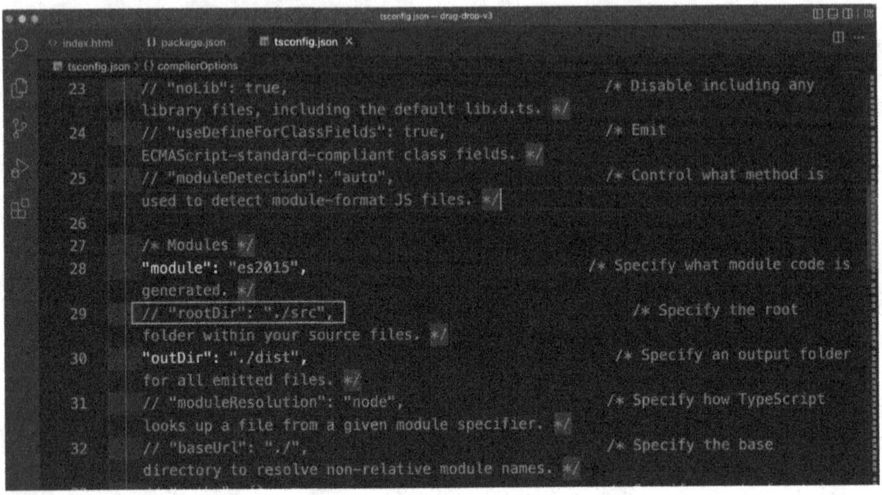

Figure 9-4. *The tsconfig.json file*

Next, you need to delete the .js from all the TypeScript files, as shown in Listing 9-12.

Listing 9-12. Deleting js from the Files

```
import { DragTarget } from "../models/drag";
import { Project, ProjectStatus } from "../models/project";
import Component from "./base";
import { prjState } from "../state/state";
import { Item } from "./item";
```

Next, create a webpack.config.js file in the root directory and add the contents of Listing 9-13 to it. You have an entry point and output details. You also have rules using regular expressions, which say to look for all the ts files. You can use ts-loader to change the TypeScript files to JavaScript and exclude the node_modules.

Listing 9-13. Creating the webpack.config.js File

```
const path = require('path');

module.exports = {
    mode: 'development',
    entry: './src/index.ts',
    output: {
        filename: 'bundle.js',
        path: path.resolve(__dirname, 'dist'),
        publicPath: 'dist'
    },
    devtool: 'inline-source-map',
    module: {
        rules: [
            {
                test: /\.ts$/,
                use: 'ts-loader',
                exclude: /node_modules/
            }
        ]
    },
    resolve: {
        extensions: ['.ts', '.js']
    }
};
```

Next, add a build script to the package.json file; it will run webpack (see Listing 9-14).

Listing 9-14. Updating package.json

```
"scripts": {
  "build": "webpack"
},
```

Delete all the folders and files inside the dist folder, as shown in Figure 9-5.

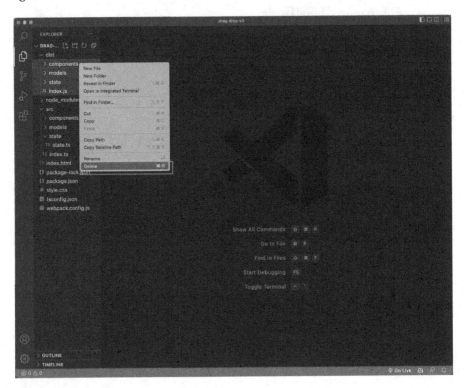

Figure 9-5. *Delete files*

Run the npm run build command from the command line. You will see the bundle.js file created in the dist folder, as shown in Figure 9-6.

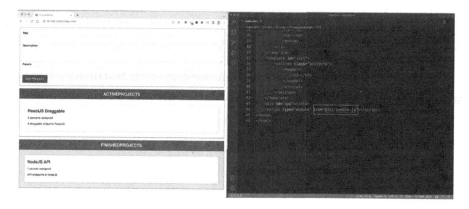

Figure 9-6. *The bundle.js file*

You also updated the script file in `index.html` to `bundle.js`. The app is running perfectly on the localhost, as shown in Figure 9-7.

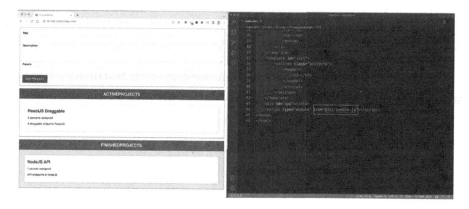

Figure 9-7. *index.html*

Now, when you open the Network tab, you will see fewer requests being made, as shown in Figure 9-8.

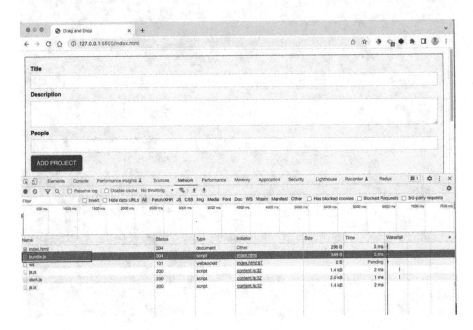

Figure 9-8. *The localhost shows fewer requests being made*

You can find the code on GitHub at `https://github.com/nabendu82/drag-drop-ts-v3`.

Summary

In this chapter, you updated the drag-and-drop project. You divided it into small, manageable modules and used webpack to make the project more efficient. In the next chapter, you will create a small party app with React and TypeScript.

CHAPTER 10

Creating a Party App in ReactJS with TypeScript

React is the most popular JavaScript library. Almost all production projects are made in ReactJS or Angular. In Angular, you have to write your code in TypeScript, but in React that is not the case.

You can easily add TypeScript to a ReactJS project by specifying it using `create-react-app`. In this chapter, you learn how to create a party app in ReactJS with TypeScript (see Figure 10-3 for the completed project).

Party App

You will create a simple party list app with React and TypeScript. Open your terminal and provide the command shown in Figure 10-1. Notice that you have to specify `--template typescript` to create a ReactJS project with TypeScript.

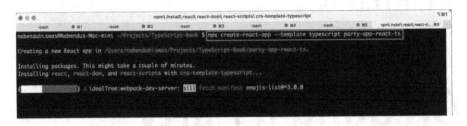

Figure 10-1. *The TypeScript template*

Listing People

Next, in the App.tsx file, create a simple state called people, using the useState hook. The only difference from a normal ReactJS component in JavaScript is that you specify the type here.

You are specifying that people is an array of objects containing name, age, img, and note. See Listing 10-1.

Listing 10-1. Creating the App.tsx File

```
import { useState } from 'react';
import './App.css';

function App() {
  const [people, setPeople] = useState<{name: string, age:
  number, img: string, note: string}[]>([
    { name: 'John',
      age: 30,
      img: 'https://randomuser.me/api/portraits/men/22.jpg',
      note: 'John is a very good person'
    },
    { name: 'Jane',
      age: 25,
      img: 'https://randomuser.me/api/portraits/women/22.jpg',
```

```
      note: 'Jane is a very good person'
    },
  ])

  return (
    <div className="App">
      <h1>People List - Birthday Party</h1>
    </div>
  );
}

export default App;
```

Next, create a components folder inside the src folder and then create the PeopleList.tsx file inside it. If you try to import this list in the App.tsx file, you would get an error because you have not defined the type. See Listing 10-2.

Listing 10-2. Adding the PeopleList.tsx File

```
import PeopleList from './components/PeopleList';

function App() {
  return (
    <div className="App">
      <h1>People List - Birthday Party</h1>
      <PeopleList people={people} />
    </div>
  );
}

export default App;
```

In the PeopleList.tsx file, you are receiving the props of people. You loop through the list using a map and showing the image, name, age, and note received from the App component. The main thing to note here is the React.FC type of the PeopleList component, which means it's a functional component.

The IProps interface tells you that you have a person with an object type inside an array. Now, all of the errors are resolved. See Listing 10-3.

Listing 10-3. Creating the PeopleList.tsx File

```
interface IProps {
    people: {
        name: string
        age: number
        img: string
        note: string
    }[]
}

const PeopleList: React.FC<IProps> = ({ people }) => {
    return (
        <ul>
            {people.map(person => (
                <li className="list">
                    <div className="list-header">
                        <img className="list-img"
                        src={person.img} />
                        <h2>{person.name}</h2>
                    </div>
                    <p>{person.age} years old</p>
                    <p className="list-note">{person.note}</p>
                </li>
            ))}
```

```
        </ul>
    )
}

export default PeopleList
```

You also need to add the styles for the component in the App.css file. See Listing 10-4.

Listing 10-4. Creating the App.css File

```css
.App {
  text-align: center;
}
.list {
  list-style: none;
  display: flex;
  align-items: center;
  width: 50rem;
  margin: 0rem auto;
  border: 0.1rem solid rgba(0, 0, 0, 0.233);
  padding: 1rem;
  justify-content: space-between;
}
.list-header {
  display: flex;
  align-items: center;
}
.list-header h2 { color: rgb(37, 36, 36)}
.list-img {
  width: 4rem;
  height: 4rem;
  border-radius: 100%;
```

```
  margin-right: 0.5rem;
}
.list-note {
  width: 30%;
  text-align: left;
}
```

Now, in the localhost, you will get both of these people, as shown in Figure 10-2.

Figure 10-2. *The localhost shows the results*

Adding People

Next, create a component called AddToPeople.tsx in the components folder. You have three input fields that take input: name, age, and img. There is also a textarea for a note. Lastly, there is a button to submit the entries.

You have an input state to take the name, age, img, and note. In handleChange, you use the common React trick, which uses e.target. name to create a common function.

The main thing to note is the e type, which is commonly known as an *event*. In this example, you have to set it to React.ChangeEvent, but it can have two other values—HTMLInputElement or HTMLTextAreaElement. See Listing 10-5.

Listing 10-5. Creating the AddToPeople.tsx File

```tsx
import React, { useState } from 'react'

const AddToPeople = () => {
    const [input, setInput] = useState({ name: "", age: "",
    note: "", img: "" })

    const handleChange = (e: React.ChangeEvent<HTMLInputElement
    | HTMLTextAreaElement>) => {
        setInput({
            ...input,
            [e.target.name]: e.target.value
        })
    }

    const handleClick = () => {}

    return (
        <div className="add-people">
            <input type="text" onChange={handleChange}
            className="add-input" name="name" value={input.
            name} placeholder="Name" />
            <input type="text" onChange={handleChange}
            className="add-input" name="age" value={input.age}
            placeholder="Age" />
            <input type="text" onChange={handleChange}
            className="add-input" name="img" value={input.img}
            placeholder="Url" />
            <textarea onChange={handleChange} className="add-
            input" name="note" value={input.note}
            placeholder="Note" />
            <button onClick={handleClick} className="add-
            button">Add to List</button>
```

```
        </div>
    )
}

export default AddToPeople
```

You can now add the styles for this new component to the App.css file. See Listing 10-6.

Listing 10-6. Adding Styles to App.css

```css
.add-people {
  display: flex;
  flex-direction: column;
  width: 30rem;
  margin: 5rem auto
}

.add-input {
  padding: 0.5rem;
  font-size: 1rem;
  margin: 0.3rem 0rem
}

.add-button {
  padding: 0.5rem;
  cursor: pointer;
  background-color: darkmagenta;
  font-weight: 700;
  color: white;
  border: none;
  border-radius: 0.5rem;
  text-transform: uppercase;
}
```

Now, you can render AddToPeople from the App.tsx file. You pass people and setPeople as props. You will get errors, because the types are expected to be given in AddToPeople.

Sometimes, it is difficult to find the types for the props. In such cases, if you hover your mouse over the props, you can see the expected types. You can copy those types from there. See Listing 10-7.

Listing 10-7. Adding AddToPeople to App.tsx

```
import AddToPeople from './components/AddToPeople';

function App() {
  ...
  return (
    <div className="App">
      <h1>People List - Birthday Party</h1>
      <PeopleList people={people} />
      <AddToPeople people={people} setPeople={setPeople} />
    </div>
  );
}

export default App;
```

Back in the AddToPeople.tsx file, you will have an interface containing the people and setPeople props. Notice that I copied the setPeople props from the copying that was done earlier. See Listing 10-8.

Listing 10-8. Adding Props to AddToPeople.tsx

```
import React, { useState } from 'react'

interface IProps {
    people: {
        name: string
        age: number
```

```
        img: string
        note: string
    }[],
    setPeople: React.Dispatch<React.SetStateAction<{
        name: string;
        age: number;
        img: string;
        note: string;
    }[]>>
}

const AddToPeople: React.FC<IProps> = ({setPeople,
people}) => {
    ...
    return (
    )
}

export default AddToPeople
```

Next, you need to update the `handleClick` function. You simply use `setPeople` and the spread operator and then pass the object with input from the user. In the end, you are setting the name, age, img, and note to empty strings. See Listing 10-9.

Listing 10-9. Adding handleClick to AddToPeople.tsx

```
const handleClick = () => {
        if(!input.name || !input.age || !input.img || !input.
        note) return;
        setPeople([...people, {name: input.name, age:
        Number(input.age), img: input.img, note: input.note}])
        setInput({ name: "", age: "", note: "", img: "" })
}
```

You can now add a new person to the localhost (see Figure 10-3). You can find the code for this process on GitHub at `https://github.com/nabendu82/party-app-react-ts`.

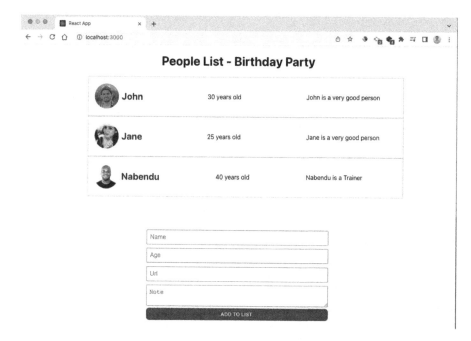

Figure 10-3. *Final app*

Summary

In this chapter, you created a party app in ReactJS with TypeScript. You learned how to add types to various parts of the React project.

In the final chapter, you are going to create a small Redux app with TypeScript.

CHAPTER 11

Using React Redux with TypeScript

In this chapter, you learn to add TypeScript to a React Redux project (see Figure 11-2 for the completed app). You need basic knowledge of Redux to follow along in this chapter.

Setting Up the Project

You will create a new React app with TypeScript by adding the template to `create-react-app`. See Figure 11-1.

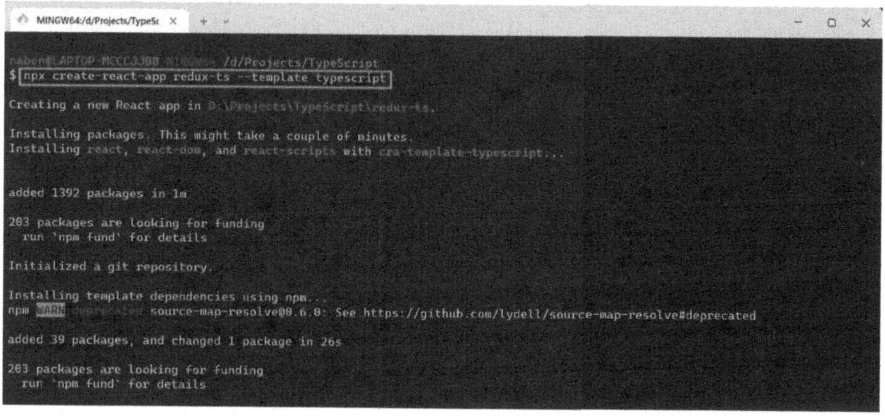

Figure 11-1. *Create a React app*

N. Biswas, *TypeScript Basics*, https://doi.org/10.1007/978-1-4842-9523-6_11

Now, create a `state` folder inside the `src` folder. Inside that folder, create three more folders—`actions`, `reducers`, and `types`. Inside the actions and types folders, create an `index.ts` file.

Inside the `reducers` folder, create a `bankReducer.ts` file. Now, in the `index.ts` file that's inside the `types` folder, export an enum called `ActionType`, where you'll create two constants. See Listing 11-1.

Listing 11-1. The index.ts file in the types Folder

```
export enum ActionType {
    DEPOSIT = "DEPOSIT",
    WITHDRAW = "WITHDRAW"
}
```

Setting Up Redux

You now need to the create types that will be used in TypeScript. So, in the `index.ts` file in the `actions` folder, create two interfaces called `DepositAction` and `WithdrawAction`. You are using `ActionType` from the types folder and specifying the `number` payload. See Listing 11-2.

Listing 11-2. The index.ts file in the actions Folder

```
import { ActionType } from "../types";
interface DepositAction {
    type: ActionType.DEPOSIT,
    payload: number
}
interface WithdrawAction {
    type: ActionType.WITHDRAW,
    payload: number
}
export type Action = DepositAction | WithdrawAction;
```

In the bankReducer.ts file, add the logic of the reducers with the usual switch statements. Provide state and action and their return types. See Listing 11-3.

Listing 11-3. The bankReducer.ts File in the reducers Folder

```
import { Action } from "../actions";
import { ActionType } from "../types";

const initialState = 0;

const reducer = (state: number = initialState, action: Action):
number => {
    switch (action.type){
        case ActionType.DEPOSIT:
            return state + action.payload;
        case ActionType.WITHDRAW:
            return state - action.payload;
        default:
            return state
    }
}

export default reducer
```

You need to install the required packages before moving forward. You can do that from the terminal, as shown in Listing 11-4.

Listing 11-4. Installing Redux

```
npm i redux react-redux react-thunk @types/react-redux
```

Next, create an index.ts file in the reducers folder. Here, you add the combineReducers logic, which is required in a Redux project. See Listing 11-5.

Listing 11-5. The index.ts File in the reducers Folder

```
import { combineReducers } from "redux";
import bankReducer from "./bankReducer"

const reducers = combineReducers({
    bank: bankReducer
})

export default reducers
```

Now, you'll create actionCreators. First create the creators folder inside the state folder and the index.ts file inside that. Note the two functions—depositMoney and withdrawMoney. You are dispatching the type and payload as usual, but you should also include the amount and dispatch types here. See Listing 11-6.

Listing 11-6. The index.ts File in the creators Folder

```
import { Dispatch } from "react"
import { Action } from "../actions"
import { ActionType } from "../types"

export const depositMoney = (amount: number) => {
    return (dispatch: Dispatch<Action>) => {
        dispatch({
            type: ActionType.DEPOSIT,
            payload: amount
        })
    }
}

export const withdrawMoney = (amount: number) => {
    return (dispatch: Dispatch<Action>) => {
        dispatch({
```

```
        type: ActionType.WITHDRAW,
        payload: amount
      })
    }
}
```

Now create a `store.ts` file inside the `state` folder. You are creating a store with reducers and adding the middleware called thunk. Since you have not installed the types for `redux-thunk` yet, you need to do it that now with the `npm i @types/redux-thunk` command, which runs from the terminal. See Listing 11-7.

Listing 11-7. The store.ts File

```
import { applyMiddleware, createStore } from "redux";
import thunk from "redux-thunk"
import reducers from "./reducers";

export const store = createStore(reducers, {},
applyMiddleware(thunk))
```

Finally, add an `index.ts` file to the `state` folder. You are exporting store and actionCreators. See Listing 11-8.

Listing 11-8. The index.ts File in the state Folder

```
export * from './store';
export * as actionCreators from "./creators";
```

The Output

You need to add Redux to the application by wrapping the root element of the app with it. So, wrap the `App` component with `Provider` and pass the store in the `index.tsx` file. See Listing 11-9.

Listing 11-9. The index.ts File

```
import ReactDOM from 'react-dom/client';
import './index.css';
import App from './App';
import { Provider } from 'react-redux';
import { store } from './state';
const root = ReactDOM.createRoot(
  document.getElementById('root') as HTMLElement
);

root.render(
  <Provider store={store}>
    <App />
  </Provider>
);
```

You also need to export the reducers type from the combineReducers file of index.ts, which is in the reducers folder. See Listing 11-10.

Listing 11-10. The index.ts File in the reducers Folder

```
import { combineReducers } from "redux";
import bankReducer from "./bankReducer"

const reducers = combineReducers({
    bank: bankReducer
})

export default reducers
export type RootState = ReturnType<typeof reducers>
```

Finally, update the App.tsx file and use the useSelector hook to get the Redux state. This example uses the useDispatch hook to dispatch the actionCreators. It also provides the required types. See Listing 11-11.

Listing 11-11. The App.tsx File

```
import { useDispatch, useSelector } from 'react-redux';
import { bindActionCreators } from 'redux';
import { actionCreators } from './state';
import { RootState } from './state/reducers';
import './App.css';

function App() {
  const amount = useSelector((state: RootState) => state.bank)
  const dispatch = useDispatch();
  const { depositMoney, withdrawMoney } = bindActionCreators
  (actionCreators, dispatch)

  return (
    <div className="App">
      <h1>{amount}</h1>
      <button onClick={() => depositMoney(1000)}>Deposit</button>
      <button onClick={() => withdrawMoney(500)}>Withdraw</button>
    </div>
  );
}
export default App;
```

When you start the React app with npm start from the terminal, you will see the app with the Deposit and Withdraw buttons working fine, as shown in Figure 11-2.

Figure 11-2. *The final app*

This completes this small app. You can find the code on GitHub at https://github.com/nabendu82/redux-ts.

Summary

In this final chapter, you created a small app in ReactJS using Redux with TypeScript. You learned how to add types to various parts of the Redux project.

Index

A, B

Abstract classes, 40, 41,
    107–111, 126
addElements function, 59
addItemToList function, 84, 85
addItemToList function, 84, 85
addListener function, 98, 99, 110
addProject function, 98, 101
Advanced classes
    abstract classes, 40
    add objects, 36
    add protected class, 35
    commented out errors, 42
    error, 42
    getter and setter, 38
    inheritance, 34
    localhost, 37
    OyoRoom class, 34
    private constructors, 42
    new Report array, 38
    Singleton object, 44
    singleton pattern, 43
    static variables, 39, 40
advancedDemo.ts, 51, 52
Advanced types
    add advanced file, 51

add file to tsconfig.json, 52
discriminated unions, 55
function overloading, 59–61
index properties, 58
initial setup, 51
intersection, 52, 53
nullish coalescing, 61, 62
type casting, 56–58
type guards, 53–55
TypeScript, 51
App.tsx file, 142, 143, 149, 158, 159

C

Classes, 29
    constructor, 31
    creates new file, 32
    index.html file, 33
    OOP languages, 29
    private and read-only
        variables, 30
    tsconfig.json file, 33
config() function, 93
configure() method, 107–109, 116
contentRender() method,
    96, 107, 113

D

Decorators
  Angular, 74
  Angular template, 74, 75
  Car Class, 71
  decoratorsDemo.ts file, 74
  employee class, 76
  factories, 73
  function, 71
  logs, 72
  property, 75, 77, 78
  setup, 69, 70
  tsconfig.json file, 70
Discriminated unions, 51, 53–56
Drag-and-drop project
  abstract class, 107–111
  directory, 87, 88
  DOM selection
    add template, 89, 91
    config() function, 93
    console log, 94, 95
    importNode(), 91
    index.html file, 89
    index.ts file, 92
    output, 93
    style.css file, 89
  draggable items, 115–122
  ES6 modules (see ES6 modules,
    drag-and-drop project)
  filtering logic
    List class, 103–105
    project class, 103
    State Class, 104
  HTML, 88
  Item class, 113
  List class, 114
  rendering list
    addProject function, 98
    bug, 102
    Input class, 101
    List class, 99, 100
    Singleton Class, 98
  template update, 112
  tsconfig.json file, 89
  Webpack (see Webpack, drag-
    and-drop project)
dragOverHandler function,
  119, 120
dragStartHandler method, 116, 118
dropHandler function, 119, 120

E

Enum types, 14, 15
ES6 modules, drag-and-
    drop project
  base.ts file creation, 126
  drag.ts file creation, 124
  enhanced project, 133
  index.ts file, 132
  input.ts file creation, 131
  item.ts file creation, 127
  list.ts file creation, 129
  state.ts file creation, 125
  update tsconfig.json file, 133
Event, 85, 146
Event listener, 57, 82, 85, 93, 116

F

Function overloading, 59–61

G, H

Generic function types, 65
Generics
    array and promise
        types, 64
    classes, 68
    generic function, 66
        issue, 66
        problem, 65
        resolve, 66
        solution, 67
    genericsDemo.ts
        file, 63, 64
    generic utility, 69
    initial setup, 63
    type constraints, 66, 67

I, J, K

Index properties, 58
Inheritance, 34
Input class, 109
Interface
    addition, 44, 45
    console, 46
    Greeting interface, 47
    interfaceDemo.ts file, 44, 45
    optional parameter, 48, 49
    read-only error, 47
Intersection types, 52, 53, 62

L

List class, 99, 103, 105, 108, 114,
    119, 129
ListenerState class, 110, 111

M

moveMammal functions, 53–55
moveProject function, 118, 120

N

Nullish coalescing, 51, 61, 62
numOrStr, 13

O

OOP languages, 29
Optionals type, 15

P, Q

Party app, ReactJS
    add PeopleList.tsx file, 143
    AddToPeople to App.tsx file, 149
    AddToPeople.tsx file, 146,
        147, 149
    App.css file, 148
    App.css file creation, 145
    App.tsx file creation, 142
    final app, 151
    handleClick to AddToPeople.
        tsx, 150
    IProps interface, 144

Party app, ReactJS (*cont.*)
  localhost, 146
  PeopleList.tsx file, 143, 144
  TypeScript template, 141, 142
Property decorators, 75, 77, 78

R

React Redux project
  App.tsx file, 159
  bankReducer.ts file, reducers
      folder, 155
  create-react-app, 153
  final app, 159
  index.ts file, 158
    actions folder, 154
    creators folder, 156
    reducers folder, 156, 158
    state folder, 157
    types folder, 154
  install redux, 155
  setup, 154–157
  store.ts file, 157
removeData function, 68
rootDir and outDir, 26, 27

S

Singleton Class, 98
Singleton object, 44
split() method, 59
StoreData class, 68
String and Boolean types,
    5, 7, 8, 19

T

To-do list project
  add events, 85
  add HTML, 81
  add items, 85
  addItemToList, 84
  index.ts file creation, 82, 83
  create snowpack project, 80
  delete files, 81
  newTask object, 83
  start project, 80
  install uuid and @types/uuid
      packages, 82
tsconfig.json file, 26
Type Casting, 56–58
Type Guards, 53–55
TypeScript
  arrays
    complex arrays with
        types, 11
    types, 11
  Boolean types, 7
  Boolean issue, 6
  console, 19, 53
  enum types, 14, 15
  functions, 12
  function types, 13
  inferences, 7, 8
  interfaces, 16
  JavaScript, 1
  limitation, 1
  literal types, 14
  live server, 3

number issue, 6

number types, 5, 6

objects

errors, 10

with no types, 9

with types, 9

optionals type, 15

party app, ReactJS (*see* Party
app, ReactJS)

project setup, 1–3

run code, 18

simple main.ts, 3

String types, 7

types, 16, 17

union types, 13, 14

TypeScript compiler

include adds the main.ts
file, 26

index.html file, 27

node_modules, 25

project, 22, 23

rootDir and outDir, 26, 27

tsc error, 24

tsc file again, without the error, 25

tsconfig.json file, 27

watch mode, 21

U, V

updateListeners function, 119

W, X, Y, Z

Watch mode, 21

Webpack, drag-and-drop project

bundle.js file, 139

create webpack.config.js
file, 136, 137

delete files, 138

index.html, 139

install, 135

delete js, 136

localhost, 140

network tab, 134, 135

tsconfig.json file, 136

update package.json file, 137, 138

Printed in the United States
by Baker & Taylor Publisher Services